THE WORD AND THE WORLD

PASTORAL STUDIES FOR THE MODERN PREACHER

BY THE

Rev. JOHN WAKEFORD, B.D.

CANON AND PRECENTOR OF LINCOLN; AND SPECIAL LECTURER IN PASTORAL
THEOLOGY IN KING'S COLLEGE, LONDON, 1911-1912

WITH A PREFACE BY THE LORD BISHOP OF LINCOLN

LONGMANS, GREEN AND CO.

39 PATERNOSTER ROW, LONDON

NEW YORK, BOMBAY AND CALCUTTA

1912

PREFACE BY THE BISHOP OF LINCOLN.

THE author of these pages invites me to prefix to them a few words by way of introduction.

If I do so, it is not because Canon Wakeford is one of the most interesting and forcible of contemporary preachers, nor because he and his have been reckoned among my friends for many years, nor yet because I have prevailed upon him to come and devote to the Diocese of Lincoln the powers he has long placed at the service of Liverpool; but because this book has the merit of setting its readers thinking, handling as it does important topics with much vigour and originality.

I do not profess agreement with the author in every particular. His way is to state an opinion strongly, with less of the qualification and reserve that some of us affect. Perhaps, too, he is more positive and dogmatic than those who have been trained to study Church doctrines and institutions from the point of view of historical evolution. But he provokes us to thought, and compels us to consider. In particular, Chapter

VI, on the influence of social and other environment in predisposing men to welcome or decline
the Gospel, struck me as quite new and worth
attentive study.

For, indeed, if the ministers of Christ be fishers
of men, then it is their business as fishermen to
acquaint themselves with the habits and movements of their shoals, and to study the best
theories of their craft.   Much labour is lost in our
ministry through inexpert methods, and method
should never become merely traditional but should
be the outcome of an alert intelligence and the
fresh experience of life.   Never was this more
necessary than in our day.

It is because these pages are so full of life and
criticism and experience, and compel reflection
upon great subjects, that I wish for them a wide
circulation.

EDWARD : LINCOLN.

2 *August*, 1912.

PREFACE.

THERE is undeniable need of increased study of
method in pastoral preaching and teaching. The
influence of the pulpit is threatened by the popularity of modern journalism, and it is no longer
sufficient to address to a congregation a monograph
or a criticism of a Scripture text. It has become
urgently necessary not only to have something to
say, but to say it in a manner that claims for it a
personal interest and carries it into its right domain
of heart and mind. The modern preacher must
know practically something of psychology and
something of sociology if he would commend his
theology to effect. These lectures, delivered as a
course in Pastoral Theology in King's College,
London, may suggest some pertinent considerations.
St. Clement of Alexandria wrote of the Christian
life as a continuous education " in an ordered succession of reasonable actions, in unbroken fulfilment of the teaching of the Word ". Our Guide
and Tutor in this life " educates the ripe scholar
by mysteries, the ordinary believer by hopes of a
better life, the hardened through corrective discipline

operating upon the senses ". The preacher, assist-
ant in the school of Christ, must know how to use
his opportunity, and press into spiritual service the
incidents and experiences which to some appear to
be accidental or trivial.

In Appendix A may be found the replies of
some of our most competent parish priests to
three questions addressed to them. Their evidence
adds much to the value of this book for all serious
students.

CONTENTS.

CHAPTER I.

REVEALED TRUTH.

CHAPTER II.

POSTULATE OF CHRISTIANITY.

CHAPTER III.

THE PROPHETIC MINISTRY.

CONTENTS

CHAPTER VII.

PERSONAL CONDITIONS.

CHAPTER VIII.

THE LIFE OF CONVERSION.

CHAPTER IX.

INSTRUCTION IN RELIGIOUS KNOWLEDGE.

CONTENTS

CHAPTER X.

CHRISTIAN DUTY.

CHAPTER I.

REVEALED TRUTH.

THE Christian faith is a coherent body of teaching. Its distinctive position is this: God Himself sent His Son into the world to teach mankind, and He has given the faith once for all to those whom He has redeemed. The four evangelists have preserved for all ages the sacred deposit. It is plain at once that for its effect in human nature the faith depends upon personal reception. Its own contents are fixed and invariable, but as it must be translated into every tongue so it needs to be interpreted and stated in terms appropriate to every class of hearers. The ministry of the Holy Spirit and the work of the Church can add nothing to the contents of revelation, but these are chiefly for the enabling of our nature to receive and respond to the Gospel. In His first parable our Lord stated the need of the prepared soul for the word of truth. The parable of the Sower, as it is commonly called, is a preface to the doctrines of Christ; in that parable He speaks of four states of the heart, the hardened, the fickle, the pre-

I

occupied, and the true.   He teaches that the Word itself can have no lasting effect unless it be received in an honest and good heart.

The word that is not mixed with faith in them that hear it is fruitless.   Too frequently it is assumed that the apparent failure in attracting people to church or in making the claims of religion to be commonly felt justifies a doubt of the truth or practical value of the Gospel. But in reading the story of the evangelists one is compelled to notice that in the days of our Lord upon earth there were many persons to whom the truth seemed to be false, whilst it came to the hearts of others as axiomatic and irresistible : the thieves on either side of the Crucified most conspicuously exemplify this difference. Closer attention shows that in every case the personal character of the hearer was the predisposing cause of acceptance or rejection when the moment came.   And this is the true worth and gravity of human experience ; by every act of volition, in matters trivial or serious, we are building up a character which is itself a capacity to receive or a prejudice to reject the Word of God. No one approaches the supreme decision of life with perfect freedom and detachment.   The great choice is the resultant of innumerable preferences and predispositions and tendencies.

We have not to alter the Word or to accommodate it to the World.   We must face rather the problem of winning for the Word its necessary reception.   That the soul of man is naturally Christian, is an ancient and true saying, but the normal man nowhere exists.   The human soul and Divine truth both issue from God, and are related to one another as light and the eye are related.   But the eye closed or filled with clay or seriously diseased makes no use of the light, and the soul needs certain conditions and circumstances to enable it to receive truth unto salvation. The study of mankind is a necessary part of our pastoral equipment; as fishers of men we must know how to cast the net so as to enclose the multitude of fishes. Men are of all sorts and conditions, that is, of various groups or companies, and of different temperaments. Forms of appeal that would commend a cause to one class of persons might repel the sympathy of others. A single event may have totally different values and characters in its several aspects. For instance, a general election is for the politician a matter of intense interest in reference to party and government; for the man of business it is an occasion of financial disturbance, of increased gains and losses; for the moralist and the preacher it usually marks a period of increased falsehood and venality in public life and lessened credit attached to public speaking. If every one as on the Day of Pentecost must hear in his own tongue the wonderful works of God we must take thought of the many conditions, often complex and confused, which limit or embarrass the soul to which the Word is to be addressed.

In every age this problem has to be faced anew. In addition to those influences which are regularly marked and noted, successive generations have different tempers and climates of thought. We are aware without argument of the possibility, for instance, of passing a law at one time which twenty years earlier must have caused a revolution. And there are definite influences and conditions with which we are bound to reckon. Of these it would be natural to make first allusion to external religious conditions. Before a man comes to the personal question of vital spiritual life he has some general attitude towards the public representations of

religion ; that attitude must in every case in some way
condition his personal reception of spiritual truth. In
alluding to these matters we are making no sentence
of praise or blame : we are noting facts as they actually
exist.

The position of the Church in this country is one
of the most important of these considerations. An
established Church is always likely to be misunderstood by the ignorant and ill-informed ; it is assumed
that the clergy are a " police of morals " employed
and commissioned by the Government. That in itself
is an assumption in this land that seriously hampers
our ministry : the Church is supposed to be of necessity in a Babylonish captivity. It is not doubted
that the clergy are sincere, but it is taken for granted
that they cannot afford to be too sincere, and it is not
expected that they will take the side that is unpopu-
lar, or identify themselves with a falling cause. Our
Church is not evidently and conspicuously free from
worldly interest and political partisanship. In the
judgment of many, apart from all financial considerations, it loses more than it gains from its misunderstood
relations with the State. To that we must add further
that the increased misunderstanding of these relations,
fostered and propagated for many years past in this
country, has put an odious character upon the Divine
Society in the minds of a considerable proportion of our
people. It is now believed by many that our Creeds
owe their existence to Acts of Parliament, that our
Church is a department of civil government, that our
Bishops derive their spiritual authority from the State.
And there are few fautors and patrons of Dissent in our
rural districts more whole-hearted and sincere than some
farmers who suppose that the tithe is a State tax which

would fall into their own pockets on a certain change of law. The established position of the Church, whatever that may be in fact, and the misrepresentation of what establishment means, have seriously prejudiced the Church in very many parts of this country. If the apparent dignity which the Church derives from that position has brought us any adherents, they are an unspeakable weakness to our spiritual character ; it is inconceivable that any devout soul would be attracted into membership by a religious body because it is tricked out with worldly honours.

And correspondingly the character and temper of Dissent must be noticed in this connexion. The existence of Nonconformity in general is advantageous to the Church ; it offers an alternative to persons who, if they had no such choice, might be aggrieved or reluctant Church members. Nonconformity ought to draw off even more commonly than it does those who refuse our discipline or reject any part of the Creed : in some measure it does in fact relieve us of elements that would embarrass us much more than open opposition. And yet further the existence of Nonconformity anywhere is a perpetual challenge, Will ye not also go away ? It ought to mean that none continue to profess Churchmanship unless it be by conviction. But whilst Nonconformity may serve the Church well in these ways, it is clear that the absolute truth of Christianity is not impressed upon them that are without by disagreements amongst Christians on matters of doctrine. It is undeniably an advantage to have a clear issue set before men. If the question were raised simply whether one should be such a follower of Christ as was St. John the Divine or St. Paul, or whether one should go away sorrowful because one has other possessions, it is probable that

few would make the mischoice.   If anyone were offered
Christianity or nothing the answer would come without
hesitation.   Nonconformity confuses the issue ; it suggests that the Gospel needs editing, and may be relieved
of much of its supernatural contents and robbed of its
imperative note.   The existence of a competitive assort-
ment of representations of the Gospel is not only a
bewilderment for one who wills to hold the truth, but
it is a statement that man chooses God rather than God
chooses man, and it consequently throws a slight upon
the Christian idea of God.

One of our most serious difficulties at this moment is
due to the grave change that has come over modern
Dissent.   The austerity and even melancholy severity of
the seventeenth-century Puritan was far more spiritual
and Christian than the complaisant and tolerant temper of the twentieth-century Dissenter.   Increasingly
we find the growth of what is called the institutional
church—a weak religious core round which are grouped
literary and debating societies, athletic and providence
clubs, and the usual apparatus of social entertainment
and recreation.   In many places a variety entertainment
on Sunday afternoon is the principal event of the week :
a proposal to keep a fast-day would be received with
astonishment and ridicule.   Dissent as a religious force
or religious influence in this country is apparently sinking ; as a political and social movement with some
admirable qualities and some other elements it may
continue for a time to exist.   In our ministry of evan-
gelizing the people we have to reckon with the difficulties created by the spiritual deterioration of other
religious agencies.   It is necessary also to reckon with
the character of local Dissent that one may direct the
appeal of the pulpit to meet or to countervail the local

bias. It is of course evident that where the alternative
to our message is Quakerism the attitude of the Dissenter towards the Church is unlike that which it would
be in a parish containing many Irish Romanists. The
Cornish Bible Christian, the East Anglian Baptist, the
West Yorkshire Quaker, the Welsh Calvinistic Methodist
have widely differing conceptions of God and of man's
salvation. It is our business to know what religious
ideas are current in the locality in which we have to
exercise our ministry.

Turning from the nominally religious influences we
find our people affected by changes in social customs and
national life. For more than forty years we have had
in this country compulsory elementary education. Perhaps the best that can be said for such a system as we
have fitfully shaped is that it discovers and advances a
certain number of naturally gifted persons who might
otherwise have died untaught and undeveloped. For
the rest we are paying dearly in morals for the trifling
gains in intelligence. The slightest inquiry into the
character of popular literature will show that the great
majority of persons who have learned to read do not
know what is worth reading. Probably no competent
judge of the matter would care to say that our daily
papers in 1912 are as well written or as well edited as
they were in 1870. The popular demand to-day is for a
lower class journalism. And our common education has
promoted a disregard of learning : persons who know how
to read the evening papers have less respect for scholarship and sound learning than they have who cannot
read or write. They suppose themselves to be learned
persons and they have lost reverence for learning. And
again our common education has had the ill-effect of
throwing too great an emphasis on mere mentality,

and morality has suffered a corresponding slight and neglect. With a general diffusion of some elementary knowledge there has come in a hysterical and neurotic temper amongst our people. They have not acquired thought or the processes of reason, but they have lost the moral instincts of self-control and devotion to duty. Such elementary teaching as Whitehall has given to our people has broken up many local traditions that were good, effaced distinctions amongst our people that were wholesome, and smothered the age-long crafts of our rural districts as hedging, ditching, and thatching. These were really of the nature of education, but that which has destroyed them is not true education.

And when we turn to the consideration of what is really true learning to-day we find that specializing, which has become common, tends to make men less ready to receive religious teaching; for the specialist usually has a disproportioned view of life, and very often the much learning of one detail of a single science has made him mad morally and spiritually. The most direct specific for a sceptical botanist, if he would come to a knowledge of the truth, is to study astronomy, and for the naturalist the most direct way to God is probably through mathematics. Modern learning tends to narrow the grasp and shorten the vision, and the Catholic Faith is offered to the largeness and wholeness of our nature.

As an illustration of this one may give the most distinguished name. Dr. Darwin, in his "Recollections of the Development of my Mind and Character," written as an autobiographical sketch for his children, records this of himself. He writes:—

"I have said that in one respect my mind has changed during the last thirty or forty years. Up to the age of thirty or beyond it, poetry of many kinds—such as the works of Milton, Gray, Byron, Wordsworth, Coleridge and Shelley—gave me great pleasure, and, even as a schoolboy, I took intense delight in Shakespeare, especially the historical plays. I have also said that formerly pictures gave me considerable—and music very great—delight. But now for many years I cannot endure to read a line of poetry; I have tried lately to read Shakespeare and found it so intolerably dull that it nauseated me. I have also almost lost my taste for pictures and music. Music generally sets me thinking too energetically on what I have been at work on instead of giving me pleasure. I retain some taste for fine scenery, but it does not cause me the exquisite delight which it formerly did. . . .

"This curious and lamentable loss of the higher æsthetic tastes is all the odder, as books on history, biographies, and travels (independently of any scientific facts which they may contain), and essays on all sorts of subjects interest me as much as ever they did.

"My mind seems to have become a kind of machine for grinding general laws out of large collections of facts, but why this should have caused the atrophy of that part of the brain alone on which the higher tastes depend I cannot conceive. A man with a mind more highly organized or better constituted than mine would not, I suppose, have thus suffered, and if I had to live my life again I would have made a rule to read some poetry and listen to some music at least once every week, for _____ the parts of my brain now atrophied would thus _____ kept active through use. The loss of these _____ loss of happiness, and may possibly be in-_____ the intellect, and more probably to the moral _____ y enfeebling the emotional part of our nature."

Further, we are living in days in which happily a certain and considerable amount of luxury is to be found everywhere.   Within 100 years past our poor-law guardians have apprenticed little girls of less than ten years of age from the workhouse to the plough, and in some of our rural districts black bread has been the staple food, and fresh meat has been used but three or four times in a year.   In some districts till within fifty years past underclothes were unknown amongst the manual workers.   Now all this is changed and our people generally have acquired, and recently acquired, comfortable conditions of life and pleasant circumstances.   It is not surprising that this has resulted in a diversion of interest, and that less thought is given to the future since the present has become so much more gratifying.   If preachers offer to their people the promise of happiness hereafter as a compensation for the disadvantages of their present state, it must be expected that with the improvement of their present state the people will become deaf to the preachers.   And we have in this day not only the wide diffusion of domestic comfort, but also a bewildering multiplication of the means and habits of social pleasure and relaxation. In our great towns music halls and rinks and picture-dromes and vaudevilles and dime-shows are obsessing the common mind of the lower trading and artisan population.   Without reference to the direct question, as to whether these entertainments are morally clean in themselves, the fact that they attract and occupy the attention of vast masses of our people habitually is un-toward and ill-boding.   The person accustome[d to] forms of amusement or recreation becomes [ ] unable to think clearly or feel truly.   It is a[ ] in our social life that any entertainments [ ] scenic character are pushing out what is called legitimate drama; this means that those who frequent public entertainments have less patience or sustained thought, and are too impatient to follow the thread of a plot. Amusements do not make a people happy; they rather induce sadness and pessimism. And this is a false note in life, and brings the soul to be bilious, petulant, and querimonious.

And close akin to this temper of pleasure-seeking is that new social vice which threatens the overthrow of the white races. The birth-rate for London in 1910 was the lowest known: from 35 in the 1000 in 1871 it has fallen to 23 in the 1000. This decrease in the birth-rate is to be found in the country as well as the towns, and even in our sparsely populated colonies. Only incidentally is this appalling state of things here noted that we may mark that where this vice is common Christianity can get no hearing. Life is a sacred gift and mystery; persons who desecrate the sanctities of our nature render themselves incapable of realizing spiritual things. The drifting away of young married people after the birth of two or three children must occasion a mental note in this connexion, and the sad hardness of married women of later age may often be due to this form of domestic harlotry.

In our country districts there is one other well-marked change with which we must reckon. Farms are being in some districts converted into grazing lands since the repeal of the Corn Laws. It results that labour is being reduced very largely and the number of labourers employed is but a fraction of the number that earned their living formerly by tillage. And the few labourers employed in the changed conditions of work have as much to occupy them on Sundays as on the other days of the week : the cattle must be tended and watered. This leaves them no opportunity for church attendance, and we see no more the rows of ploughmen or harvesters that used to keep Sunday quietly and seriously, attending church twice in the day. You may regard any person whose public religious exercise is limited to Sunday evening as virtually lost to the Church ; that habit does not satisfy the sacramental necessities, whilst it does suffice to put off the personal sense of the need of religion. It is hard to find in some of our rural districts the settled village Church life that ought to be a common factor of our national character. Restlessness and low-class journalism have come into our remotest hamlets disturbing and poisoning the contentment and simplicity of our people. True home life is less common both in town and country ; the feverish haste to be rich, and the pretentiousness which is the ordinary modern form of vulgarity, the sick hurry of to-day present us with difficulties to which we must address ourselves studiously.

The evangelical revival of the eighteenth century owed much to continental movements ; the French Revolution was a sufficient comment on the " Rights of Man," and the fifteenth and sixteenth chapters of the " Decline and Fall of the Roman Empire" were answered by contemporary history. So it has been remarked a serious period usually is found to follow an exhausting war, and after a great national disaster there is undeniably a new opportunity. But such opportunities must be used with the utmost care and restraint, for excitement or horror may tend to immediate moral unrestraint and subsequent hardening and indifference. The burning of a theatre with the loss of one hundred lives in an English city twenty years ago probably advanced the spiritual life of none ; but it had surprising moral results. For six or seven days following the calamity the people of the city were horror-stricken, aghast, taciturn, and then came the reaction—an outburst of drunkenness and abandonment. It is a very safe rule that any excess of feeling threatens to destroy the spiritual disposition ; intense poverty or excessive wealth, intolerable pain or unbroken pleasure, great victories or crushing defeats do not promote generally the reception of the Gospel. The ordinary tenor of life with its common circumstances and duties, with its opportunities and experiences, in which man finds himself moved to think and to feel through all the gamut of love and hate, affords the best conditions for disposing the soul to hear the Word. It is for us to address the Word to the soul with a sympathetic knowledge of those circumstances which determine the personal character.

Consider, for instance, the method of St. Paul the great missionary. With the Roman citizenship and Greek training he found himself charged with the planting of Christianity in Asia Minor and Eastern Europe. With spiritual insight and instinct he made his two longest residences in Corinth and Ephesus ; these were the greatest centres of popular movement on sea and on land affecting that whole area. In each of these places he settled down for long sustained periods and taught moving multitudes ; he cast the Bread of Life indeed on the waters as he preached to thousands coming and going. But he made his influence upon that area still more complete by his association with Thessalonica, the centre of official traffic in that region. Corinth stood for commerce, Ephesus for religion, and Thessalonica for political movement in St. Paul's field of missions; with the sagacity of a statesman and the alertness of a soldier he knew the value of those great points of influence.

We note the conditions of modern life not that we may despair or complain nor even that we may condemn. They are of interest to us here only as they help us to shape our message and direct our appeal. We note them not by way of saying that these things are evil or hostile to our work, but that we may take counsel how best to do our work in the circumstances in which our lot is cast. Let us be confident that with all that shifts, of custom and apparent chance, and social climate or personal atmosphere, the Word that we have to deliver is the Word of unchangeable truth, and will find its due reception in the heart of man.

It is incontestable that there are many advantages in modern life for the preacher of the Gospel. We are no longer called to affirm the existence of God in the face of a world all-sceptical. The atheist is not to be found amongst intelligent people to-day; though infidelity, that is to say unfaithfulness to one's convictions, is very common. But further, and it is a great way further, we have not to argue the unity of the Godhead; that too is commonly acknowledged by modern intelligence. For extended science has brought home to us all the pervading unity of nature, and a plurality of gods has become unthinkable. Even the fool has said in his heart there is one God, and in this matter our labours are lightened. If you compare the sermons of Dr. Liddon in St. Paul's with those delivered by M. L'Abbé Monsarbre in Notre Dame, or with the addresses of Fra Agostino of Montrafelto in Florence, you will notice that these two latter labour to establish the existence of a Supreme Being or a First Cause, whilst our English preacher begins much further on with his audience; he may confidently assume certain elementary truths to be already in possession. And since the days of Dr. Liddon there are further contentions that have passed out of existence; and we have to address ourselves to persons who already accept as axiomatic much that was formerly denied or debated. Our task is not, it may be, less difficult, but it differs definitely from theirs who found themselves called to deal with blank atheism or with that stupidity which prefers to call itself agnosticism. The mental and even the moral processes are not to be confused with the spiritual, but they may conduce to the spiritual, and well ordered they form the apparatus of spiritual reception and apprehension. The wireless telegram that passes through space is not the work of plumber or carpenter; but these artisans shape and set up the mechanical structures which transmit and receive the mysterious messages that lie without the range of their handicraft. So the man equipped and prepared in mind and soul becomes a vessel of Divine truth, and the Gospel finds the heart of the hearer and is a power unto salvation.

When God created man He gave him those circumstances which would best conduce to moral development and self-realization. These were of three characters, social life, work, and moral choice. In Eden our first parents were under these three disciplines of love and duty and temptation; every one of these influences had its necessary place in the evolution of a perfect manhood. And in modern life the absence of any one of these three conditions imperils moral character. The family life is the best home of character, and work, definite and necessary, whilst it is yet neither toilsome nor servile, is the best stimulant of moral progress and ordered habit; whilst temptation, with its

alternative possibilities of rising or sinking, is the necessary insistent note of responsibility to the will and
conscience. The young man about town in rooms and
lodging, or the idler of independent fortune who has no
need to work, or the person of sheltered life who has
no great decisions to make, a child of forty or fifty years
of age living at home, all represent to us the poverty of
character which comes of lack of these divinely appointed
circumstances. Fortunately there are very few who of
necessity must live in such defective conditions; ordinary human life is still endowed with the opportunities
that Eden offered, and to love, to work, and to choose,
are the ordinary ways by which character is produced
and strengthened.

Disciplined character is the best vessel of spiritual
truth, most receptive and most retentive. Contrast
the missions of St. Paul at Athens and at Corinth.
From the religious point of view, comparing the re-
spective devotions of these two cities, it might seem
that Athens would be an easier field than Corinth for
the Gospel. In Corinth the worship of Venus was
characterized by strange licentiousness, whilst at Athens
the worship of the gods was surprisingly devoted. But
it was at Corinth and not at Athens that the Gospel
took root and bore fruit, for in Athens the people were
leisured philosophers and those of Corinth were full of
business and industry It is not without significance
that at the Nativity the angels' proclamation was
given to shepherds who watched their flocks by
night, the only men at that moment awake and at
work. The ordinary conditions of human life will
best dispose the soul to hear the Gospel, and if ever
extraordinary means are used as, for instance, in a
mission or revival, it is that the ordinary way may be

resumed with a new sense of its advantages and opportunities.

The Word has to be brought into application to the soul, and the soul has to be brought into relation with the Word. These are the two fixed and invariable quantities, the Gospel and the soul; they do not shift or change in character or worth. But we have to consider the mode of approach and the means of reception, the establishment of that living union whereby the soul is illuminated and fertilized.

CHAPTER II.

POSTULATE OF CHRISTIANITY.

Public Discourses of Christ—His Appeal always Personal—Himself Accessible to All—Wholeness of Vision—Proportion of Truth—The Natural man and the Spiritual—Ministry of Discipline—Imperative of Christ—Necessary Renunciations—Persuasion and Dissuasion—Divine Authority of Christ—Mission of Christ—The Gospel of the Kingdom—The Personal Dilemma—The Personal Indorsement—Reception of Truth—Result of Reception.

THE teaching of our Lord is based upon His claim; He postulates that He is God. His life and teaching are evidently one: there is no mere harmony but a true identity of the Messenger and the message. Isolated passages shredded from the context of His character and their occasion cannot represent His teaching faithfully. He used human speech as one of many consistent utterances of the Godhead. To receive His words in their true sense the hearer must accept His Divine claim, and relate His words to His works, and both His words and His works to His person and His mission.

The public discourses of Christ have not the oratorical form of general addresses; His audience, however numerous, was never a crowd. He spoke as One in the confidence of, and in sympathy with, every one that heard His voice; and to every one apart and alone, however closely the multitude trod one upon another, that voice of conviction and persuasion came. The early tradition of the Church records that when Jesus stooped and wrote upon the ground, apparently answering nothing to the passionate charges brought against a woman by the Scribes and Pharisees, every man present read in that writing on the Temple floor the discovery of his own secret sin. And we may believe that the spoken words of our Lord had the same piercing and singular quality as the written words. In a manner evidently personal and particular He took up the thread of the Divine argument when He halted before the toll-gate of Levi, and stood beneath the sycamore of Zacchæus, and awoke in Nathanael the memory of his past heart-searchings. The Shepherd was always leaving the ninety and nine and seeking the one. It follows that there cannot be found in the discourses of our Lord any reference to that community of feeling and sympathy which animates and sometimes dominates a great multitude. He withdrew Himself not only from threatened death but also from promised popularity. As at one time He would not suffer Himself to be stoned so at another time He would not suffer Himself to be crowned. He knew what was in man, and He distrusted the contagion, the irresponsibility, and the fickleness of popular action. He noted that one man alone, though a Samaritan, was freer to obey his best convictions and follow his highest impulses than nine men together. Though truly in secret He taught nothing, and made no difference of public and esoteric doctrine, yet it was when they were alone, or when they had gone into a house, that He expounded all things to His disciples. The Father had committed all things to the Son, and the Son Himself taught people as they were able to bear it, careful as Jacob that no one of the flock should be hurried or over-driven.

It may be further remarked that our Blessed Lord made Himself equally accessible to all. It is not necessary to say that He received publicans and sinners, and was Himself their guest; but it is an imperfect recognition of the universality of His mission which allows it to be forgotten that He went to the feast prepared for Him by the Pharisee, and later claimed burial in the tomb of a prince of Israel. The timidity of Nicodemus, who came to Jesus by night, did not rob him of the boon granted to his humility. It was much that he overcame all the natural obstacles and deferred, the old man to the young man, the rich man to the poor man, the counsellor to the wanderer. Christ indeed set Himself in the very midst of the human race, both hearing them and asking them questions. When it was said of Him in bitter condemnation that He was a Samaritan, and had a devil, He denied that He had a devil, but answered nothing to the graver accusation. He allowed no barrier of race, or tribe, or rank, to lie between Him and the souls of men. He reckoned with privileges and with disadvantages, and in His Divine wisdom so redressed the ill-balance of social convention, and custom, and order, as to make Himself equally near to all who sought through Him to the Father. His disciples marvelled that He talked with a woman, the Pharisees that He accepted the homage of a notorious sinner; but in the personal ministry of Jesus Christ lies the spring of St. Paul's declaration, " there is neither Jew nor Greek, there is neither bond nor free, there is neither male nor female: for ye are all one in Christ Jesus ". He did not suffer the sons of Zebedee to appropriate Him, nor St. Peter to direct or over-rule His purpose; He is in very truth the Son of Mankind, and the Saviour of the world. His attitude and bearing

towards Caiaphas who spiritually would not, and towards Herod who morally could not, and towards
Pontius Pilate who incidentally did not know Him as
God illustrate the discerning and dividing nature of His
ministry; on another plane it is seen in the life of action
and parable in Galilee, beside the Messianic interpretations and fulfilments in Judea.

Again we note that the teachings of Christ link up,
unify, and associate the natural with the spiritual, the
temporal with the eternal, the human with the Divine.
His parables had this incidental purpose: they claimed
the commonplace, not only as illustrating for the
moment a lesson, but also as an association of thought
by which the lesson itself was to be recalled in the
ordinary experiences of life. In the house at Capernaum,
where He healed the palsied man, He used a phrase that
may be supplied on many later occasions—" but that
ye may know ". This word claimed the external and
visible action as the proof and exposition of the higher,
the invisible. There is always one danger besetting religious ideas: they recede from the practical in the
foreground and waste into a haze, becoming unsub-
stantial, remote, and ineffective. In Japan the artist
helps the imagination of those who view his picture by
putting simply in front of the canvas some object which
relates to the subject of the painting. For instance a
broken sword might be placed before a battle-piece, a
coiled rope or small anchor in front of a picture of a
shipwreck. It is a true artistic sense which so helps
the spectator to get depth and focus, and the atmosphere of reality and objectivity. So our Lord, when
men asked of the kingdom of heaven, took a child and
set him in the midst, and when they asked of foreign
tribute He demanded the familiar coin, and when they

spoke of the controversies of the schools on commandments, light and weighty, He pointed to the *tephallim*
on their foreheads.

He refused to discuss abstract questions: He was
not teaching philosophy, or even theology directly. He
preached salvation, and showed how man can be justified
with God. If man is to be brought into lasting relations
with God he needs to be transformed. No theory of sin
or of pardon, which leaves man unchanged in character,
will suffice as a religion. In Christ God reconciled
man to Himself; and man reconciled to God is a new
creature, a spiritual being, and a disciplined being. Our
Lord so taught His disciples as to enable them to put
a spiritual interpretation upon life. The natural man
looks on the things which are seen, and does not know
these to be, as they really are, the symbols of the unseen.
The natural man instinctively regards the course that is
run between birth and death as the whole scope of life,
and does not live as an immortal. The natural man
assumes that the universe is a physical mechanism, or a
complexity of blind and uncaused forces, and does not
know it to be under personal government, the creature
and subject of the Divine will. Our Lord in His teaching showed without argument the immediate relationship of all things to God; He opened the eyes of the
spiritually blind, and made the morally lame to walk in
the heavenward way.

And, as He taught, He encouraged a personal confidence in God, and set up an intercourse and interaction between the soul and God. He induced men to
take hold of truth and to prove its worth in the development of character. He awakened a new order
of affection in the soul, drawing the heart toward God.
All this necessitated profound and extensive changes of

temper and of purpose in those whom our Lord was
calling into the kingdom; and the demand that He
made upon men is nowhere minimized in the Gospel.
He used familiar ways to approach men, teaching by
parables and claiming the natural affections, but He
insisted that they should respond to Him along unfamiliar ways and in face of difficulties.

In every man severally there was something akin to
the Spirit of Christ, but this itself was beset and overlaid and embarrassed by the predispositions of a carnal
nature and the obsessions of evil.   Beside the ministry
of attraction which our Lord offered to the human soul
was a ministry of discipline no less necessary for fallen
man.   The expostulation of the Jews, How long makest
Thou us to doubt? is very suggestive.   Men are impatient
of long-drawn-out debate, and break away without con-
clusion, but God in Christ refused to give a formula of
religion, and drove men to thinking, that thought might
shape into conviction, and conviction build into character.   At the well of Sychar our Lord talked with a
Samaritan woman; and what seemed at first a dry
discussion of the claims of rival religions presently involved husband and household and fellow-townsmen,
and in the words of the woman, " all that ever I did ".
How long makest Thou us to doubt? is the expression
of impatience when souls find themselves compelled to
reckon with conscience as well as passion, and a memory
that will not be cheated or put off, and the experiences
of life with its penalties for wilfulness and its undeniable
mercies and blessings.

In the presence of Christ men knew their highest
and their lowest, and this made them to doubt.   The
preparatory ministry of St. John the Baptist was for
the unsettlement of a people unready to listen to God

because they were confident of themselves. They said within themselves that they were children of Abraham. They relied upon the tradition and custom of national religion; and St. John offered them such terms as they were accustomed to offer to Gentile proselytes. "Think not," he cried, "to say to yourselves we have Abraham to our father; put no confidence in religious habit or religious phrase; stones may live by the direct Word of God as men may die without it." To accept the baptism of St. John was to acknowledge that one came before God as an alien and a penitent.

And the ministry of Christ enforced the same lessons; His denunciations were directed against the complacency of those who thought they were righteous and despised others. He laboured to break up the false foundations, upon which men built the fabric of a fair exterior without regard to the all-seeing Father. He insisted that His disciples should pass through the refinement of discipline and conflict with public opinion and popular goodwill. He taught them that the praise of men must always suggest a suspicion of unfaithfulness to God, that the world's approval should always move one to self-examination in prospect of the Judgment. Before He accepted the confession of His Apostles—"Thou art the Christ," He made them recall to mind the opinions of others higher in worldly station and social rank than themselves. If their profession of faith in Him was worth His acceptance it must be no mere echo of what was said elsewhere. When He commends one as not far from the kingdom of God it is because, though a Scribe, he has broken through the wrappings of phrase and convention, and has laid hold of the truth within. His most plain disclosure of Himself as the Son of God was made to a poor man who had been born

blind, and who clung tenaciously to his confidence in
the Lightbringer, in spite of the cowardice of his
parents, the anger of the Pharisees, and the loss of his
privileges in the Synagogue. He denied indeed that
men who had settled down to receive honour of one
another could believe in God and His Son; to break
the law and face its penalty was not in His mind so
irrevocably far from the doing of the will of God as the
cultivation of a petty system of professions and evasions
by which the law seemed to be kept whilst its meaning
was lost. It is said that when Christ saw a man
ploughing on the Sabbath Day He addressed him—" O
man, if thou knowest what thou doest blessed art thou;
if thou knowest not thou art cursed ". In His parable
of the Unjust Judge He summarized all motives in three
groups, the fear of God, regard for man, and self-
interest; He knew all that was in man, and marked
how easily religion fell to the level of social convention,
and how readily social convention fell to the practice of
self-indulgence. His ministry unsettled the confidence
of the people in themselves and their rulers. The rulers
feared the overthrow of their whole nation if they let
this Man alone; the people of Jerusalem questioned
whether the rulers knew indeed that this was the
Christ.

The effect of His teaching is seen in the unfeigned
self-distrust of His Apostles when He announced to
them that one of them should be a traitor; they began
eagerly to ask, " Is it I, is it I?" The root of man's
revolt from God was in the will; the succession of evil
continually renewed in every generation was in the will
alienated from God. The conflict of the human will
with the Divine will is sin. In Christ the natures
human and Divine found their harmony, in the com-

plete response of the human will to the Divine mission. The Monothelite heresy threatened the overthrow of the Christian faith by denying the existence of the human will in Christ Jesus. It is from the harmony of the two natures in Him that there outflows into the whole Body of the Redeemed that principle of absolute obedience which is the central force of Christian character.

The Incarnation has its normal consequence in the doing of the will of God by those who are called in Christ. His teachings are such illuminations of the heart as enable men to judge whether they do well in lives of sin and waywardness. His appeals are always to that power of self-determination which God first bestowed upon man in his creation and which He did not withdraw from fallen man. Human nature had been perverted from God in disobedience: Jesus Christ came to convert man, and to reconstruct man in harmony with the will of the Father. He set Himself to rectify the human will, reckoning with the conditions of habit and prejudice and caprice and cowardice by which that will was beset. As the Prophet and Teacher of mankind, His mission was to arrest and to redirect the current of human thought and the tendency of human life. His first miracle was not only a sign of power, it was also a declaration of purpose. He came to transform, as at Cana water into wine, so everywhere the earthly into the heavenly, the carnal into the spiritual, the human into the Divine. And as at Cana the obedience of the servants was the first necessity, so now the co-operation of man's will is the prerequisite of the great work which God would do in him. In Christ God has once more set before men the necessity of decision, of choice between good and evil; He has made the issue

clear, showing us the beauty of holiness and unmask-
ing the infamy of sin.   His warnings and persuasions
countervail and neutralize the conditions which clog the
movements of the will.

Jesus Christ offered men no secondary reason for
following Him, nor availed Himself of any ordinary
human motive to bring disciples into His kingdom.
He restrained men from impulsive decisions and passionate enthusiasms.   He required of every man self-
denial as a capacity for discipleship, and He knew that
self-denial could only come of set purpose and not of
momentary impulse.   He would not suffer any man to
follow Him on false motives.   His words and actions
made it impossible for any sect of the Jews to claim
Him as theirs.   When men offered Him allegiance with
conditions He refused their allegiance.   Some asked
Him for a sign from heaven and He gave no sign.
One desired to follow Him as soon as he had discharged
another duty which conflicted with the call of Christ
and the Lord bade him follow without delay or hesitation.   His call was imperative and uncompromising;
He left no place for neutrality or indecision.   Whilst
He invited men to make the great surrender, He did
not offer any flattery to their reason by advancing arguments or giving explanations.   He spoke as One Who
feared rather lest any should come to Him irresolute
and later fall away.   He constantly disentangled the
cords by which He drew men from the threads and
clues which ran through social and political life.   He ex-
posed men to themselves: "Ye seek Me, not because ye
knew My sign, but because of the loaves".   He refused
recognition as a divider or ruler over men: He declined
the salutation of one who called Him "Good Master":
He offered no earthly advantage or social improvement

or worldly reward to His followers. Men found it pro-
portionately difficult to accept Him in the measure in
which they had received the good things of this life.
When they were filled with bread, even at His hands,
He allowed a night to pass and a journey to intervene
before He began to teach them the doctrines which His
miracle was to illustrate. His most exacting demands
were laid upon one who seems to have been touched
and drawn to Him by the fair beauty of the scene when
Jesus blessed the little children ; it is to him that our
Lord said, " Go, sell all that thou hast, and give to the
poor, and then come and follow Me ".

When people crowded about Him in Galilee, in the
days of His first popularity, He shocked their religious
prejudices and drove them from Him with the word,
" Ye must eat My Flesh and drink My Blood ". When
later some clung to Him with more deliberate prudence
He sifted them with the alternative, " Whosoever will
save his life shall lose it ". And when others, more
faithful and fervent yet, continued with Him He checked
them with the startling condition, " If any man hate not
his father and mother he is not worthy of Me, he cannot
be My disciple ". His demand was always for whole-
heartedness without compromise and without condition,
" Forsake all, take up thy cross daily and follow Me ".
On such terms only will He retain those who claim
Him as Master. When multitudes fell away, He urged
the few that remained faithful to reconsider their position and question whether they too would not depart.
He came as One Whose fan was in His hand, and He
would throughly purge His floor. All that the world
would advance of prudence and reason and sentiment and
passion was set in array against the Word of God, and on
the side of God's Word Christ enlisted and allowed no ac-

cidental alliance of the flesh or of Satan. Hard sayings that none could bear but those whose hearts God had touched, and who had been drawn by the Son to the Father, drove from Him those who could not drink His cup and be baptized with His baptism. In Galilee He steadfastly refused emotional affection and demanded resolute confidence. He withdrew from the excited populace, and He bade devils that saluted Him to hold their peace. When ten lepers clamoured to Him for cleansing He sent them away to find His blessing gradually on the road that no public demonstration might follow so great an act of healing. He never brought in spiritual things as a side issue or appealed to any passion of cupidity or avarice or patriotism or indignation. He presented before every one whom He would call into the kingdom the clear issue in which there was always something to be left or lost if Christ were chosen and claimed. He made for many a separation, a detachment, in which the soul apart might come without the disturbances and distractions of life directly under the great forces of eternity. Sometimes men are most helped by being compelled to confront harsh dilemmas, at other times by being kept from hasty formulations of doubts and difficulties: Christ dealt with every man in his need and according to his personal conditions, as when He took one aside from the multitude, or as when He led the blind man out of the town and made him then to see all things clearly.

Christ dealt with human souls through those channels of approach which practical experiences had formed and opened. Teaching by parable is the very type of this ministry; in that teaching Christ used the common thought of His hearers and their knowledge of natural things to show them the kingdom of heaven and the

truth of God.   With Divine insight He claimed the
way that lay straight to the heart; the military discipline of the centurion, the guilelessness of Nathanael,
the natural affection of parents for children, the ven-
eration of just men for the law, all were made to
serve His purpose; by all these means and such means
He reached the hearts of men.   The guileless, the
innocent, the disciplined, the penitent, the outcast,
the heart-broken, knew Him as their Kinsman in some
mysterious manner, and recognized instinctively His
truth and His claim.   But none that heard Him could
respond again without pain or cost; there was always
the renunciation, the birth-pang of the new life, the
translation out of darkness into light.   He demanded
that the kingdom of heaven should be taken by force,
that men should come to Him in face of difficulties, and
feelings in revolt, and through estrangements and for-
feitures of much to which men would naturally cling.
The Christian faith is not demonstrable but needs for its
reception in every soul an act of confidence, a movement
which over-leaps a barrier or spans a gulf, and the
Author of the faith withdrew Himself always just beyond the reach of merely natural approach.   He led
souls on to the resolution, " Henceforth know I no man
after the flesh, nay not even Christ after the flesh ".

It is evident that Christ claimed to speak with authority.   His teachings were not offered to men as
suggestions or as counsels.   They were to be received
on the ground of His authority; His moral *dicta* were
self-evident truths, and did not need the support of
miracle.   But He could not be content to stand as a
moral teacher, and His higher claim needed to be com-
mended by signs from heaven.   The words that were
Divine were attested by the works that were Divine.

The authority of Christ was not the formal authority of rulers and rabbis; He taught not as the scribes. The nature of His claim to be heard is evident in His answer to the cavil of the chief priests and scribes and elders, " By what authority doest Thou these things ? " He replied by referring them back to the baptism of John ; He asked whether his ministry was of human or Divine origin. It is not that He may claim liberty to do another irregular work. It is rather that He may associate Himself with the most real convictions that His opponents had ever known. He takes them back in thought to that occasion in their lives when formalism had broken down, and the spiritual was known as the real and the momentous. He asks in fact, Will you acknowledge the validity of your own spiritual life when you were touched to effect? in rejecting Me you are denying what you know to be your own truest and surest experience of religion.

And similarly our Lord dealt with Nathanael who approached Him with apparent hesitation; his doubts were dispelled and his heart claimed by Christ's immediate reference to the solitude and meditation of the previous day, a movement of the spirit of Nathanael which God alone shared. And again similarly Christ after His Resurrection claimed St. Thomas ; He responded personally and adequately to the necessities of the disciple who needed some support for his failing faith. The confession of St. Thomas is the acknowledgment of a heart met in its needs and won by the condescension of God.

It is the heart of man that stirs and responds to the call of Christ. He quickened a new perception and power in the soul, and drew His disciples into a confidence in God. He reached men where they were

and led them to the new life, not merely a moral life
but the spiritual and the eternal. The witness of the
Samaritans expresses the directness and force of His
claim, "We have heard Him ourselves and know that
this is the Christ". And this is still true in our own
day; whilst we whole-heartedly accept the Gospel narrative we generally feel that the miracles have their
place of necessity in the life of God living as Man
amongst men, but they do not weigh greatly in the
arguments that compel our reception of the faith. We
are increasingly constrained by the direct Word; in
His light we see light, and become obedient to the
heavenly vision.

The ministry of Christ kindled in the hearts of men
a desire for God. He knew what was in man, the
hidden treasure for which He bought the field of
human nature; He saw the worth which sin had ob-
scured and hidden. As Hilkiah the priest found, when
they purged the Temple, the book of the Law of God,
so in the cleansing of the heart of man Christ un-
covered the purpose of God. Obedience is the instinctive response of man to God when God is known
in Christ, and the Master accepted nothing less of
His disciples. Man is not effectively reached by the
Gospel until he is brought into a response to the
Divine purpose; and the fall is not retrieved unless
man lives to do the will of God. But obedience itself
presses further to become spiritual capacity and spiritual faculty. The miracles of our Lord, acts of Divine
power, were in many instances dependent upon the
co-operation of those whom He would bless. In many
cases His supernatural help had to be claimed by some
act of obedience: the ten lepers that went from Him
still leprous, the blind man that groped his way to-

wards the Pool of Siloam, the servants at Cana that drew out water at His word are instances of this kind.

He that will do the will of God shall know of the doctrine, and obedience is the medium of knowledge. We are responsible for our convictions since conduct itself is the vehicle through which enlightenments come into the understanding. In ordinary bone formation there are two distinct kinds of substance: the outer, hard and dense, forms a sheath of compact tissue, and the inner, light and porous, is spongy tissue. In surgical matters the outer sheath is of most moment; if this be splintered a complete rehabilitation is impossible. But on the other hand the inner substance may recover itself normally if the compact tissue is not shattered. And similarly conviction may make good its growth under the protecting sheath of well-ordered conduct. If Christianity were only a philosophy it might be entirely contained within the terms of the intellectual; but since it is that religion which claims the whole man for its sphere and expression it needs the whole man for its reception. Any practical response to the authority of Christ, any act of recognition of His Divinity, gives the soul an immediate access of spiritual understanding.

And in the deepening of spiritual character the knowledge of God becomes so immediate and intimate as to need less and less the intervening terms of speech and hearing, of sign and external form. In the moment in which the two disciples at Emmaus knew their Lord and recognized Him in the breaking of bread, He vanished out of their sight. So God teaches us to use the external and visible as *media* which discharge a temporary service. If these considerations are true the answer that any man gives to the question,

3

What is the nature of the authority of Christ? denotes the position of that man in the discipleship. The soul's advance is along a line in which Christ is successively Prophet, Master, Companion, Bridegroom. Probably no two ardent disciples of the Lord, if gifted with absolute facility of speech, would define their relations with Him in the same words. But facility of speech is that which is increasingly wanting as the experience of the disciple extends. The knowledge of God becomes not only direct and immediate but also incommunicable. The authority of Christ and the inspiration of the Scriptures are less the subjects of definition as they are more intuitively recognized as actual by the spiritual consciousness.

The mission of Christ was the relating of man to God. The Incarnation and the Atonement are the necessary Divine acts to accomplish this; and the radical change of heart and mind in man is the necessary subjective condition. The man in grace is the man effectively receptive of Christ's mission, and consequently responsive to God's will. The teaching mission of our Lord is wholly directed to the establishment of confidence in God. Christ is the mediator of the covenant of grace, the daysman between God and man who lays His hand upon both. The Incarnation has been thought of as the final act in the advancing order of creation, the crown in the ascending scale which moved up from chaos to cosmos. In that act humanity is assumed by the Son of God that the human may be gathered into the Divine. This is the mission of our Lord, and for this purpose the Holy Ghost is given and the Church exists.

CHAPTER III.

THE PROPHETIC MINISTRY.

Priest and Prophet—Seer and Utterer—Heralds of the Kingdom—Mission of the Church—Choice of the Twelve—Training of the Twelve—Qualifications of the Prophet—Warning and Teaching—A Diocesan Order—Austerity and Detachment—Simplicity and Restraint—Personal Dispositions—The Context of Life—Momentousness of Spiritual Truth—The Personal Appeal.

THE word Christ is used in the Old Testament of prophets, priests, and kings. Of these three offices kingship was accidental and temporary. The rabbis have always counted the wilderness the mother of their religion, and kingship was of later origin; and then demanded by the people and not appointed of God. Moses and Aaron were prophet and priest of the people in the wilderness; the Aaronic line ran in natural generation from father to son age after age, and a certain ordination by the laying on of hands passed from Moses to Joshua and the later leaders of Israel. Kingship came not by Divine appointment but in imitation of the heathen nations that surrounded Israel in Canaan. And the functions of kingship were for the most part abstracted from the sacred offices of priest and prophet. The words of Samuel as he reproached the people give us this measure of the nation's apostasy. Your sons will become soldiers and your daughters confectioners when you have made you a king, is the warning of Samuel. Political power must rest upon force or concession. As a nation the Hebrews had been shaped and

3 *

unified by revealed truth and national religion ; their impatient desire for visible monarchy showed a marked deterioration and loss of ideal.   And through their kings came almost all their later calamities, and at last the division of the two kingdoms north and south, the provision of false gods for the northern kingdom, and the wars which finally brought all the tribes into captivity.   And Herod represented kingship in Judea when the Redeemer was born in Bethlehem.

Our Lord came, the Apostle of the Father and the High Priest of humanity, to fulfil all that was foreshadowed in the two lines of Divine appointment which began with Moses and Aaron ; and when His kingly claim was challenged by Pontius Pilate, Art Thou a king then ?   He answered, To this end was I born, and for this cause came I into the world ; that I might bear witness to the truth. It is as though He reaffirmed that the prophetic office includes in its greater extent all royalty; the Truth-bearer is the true leader of true men.   And as priesthood and prophecy in the Old Covenant led up to Christ, so from Him in the New Covenant these lines run on unceasingly.   The prophetic office in the Church to-day is a natural and necessary outflow of the Incarnation. Christ is the one Rabbi of the Christian Church, and His ministers bear witness to Him through all the ages, warning every man and teaching every man that they may present every man in Christ Jesus.   In taking human nature the Son of God claimed the human race for Himself and made our nature to be the instrument of our salvation.   All that are called into the kingdom of grace must become the medium through which others are reached and claimed.

It is clear that the formation of a Divine society upon earth is the primary purpose of the mission of Christ.

He gathered men about Him and made a definite and visible society to carry revealed truth from generation to generation. He appointed for that society a duly ordered constitution, with a sacrament of initiation and a sacrament of sustenance in the fellowship. He set within that society certain officers with prescribed duties. The society exists in its integrity or completeness to express and to fulfil the will of God as revealed in Jesus Christ.

The Master evidently chose certain men to be heralds of the kingdom, prophets of the new dispensation; we need to prepare ourselves if we would fulfil this ministry. In the Old Testament the title "man of God" denoted a prophet, and St. Paul uses this title of a Christian bishop, St. Timothy. We may learn then from the Old Testament something of the prophetic ministry. A note in the first book of Samuel tells us that prophets were called seers before time in Israel, and the words *seer* and *prophet* have distinct and separate values. The Hebrew word for seer signifies a person who has second sight, spiritual clairvoyance, whilst the Hebrew word for prophet denotes an utterer who cannot forbear to speak. Correspondingly in the new dispensation the prophet must have two qualities—spiritual vision and compelling conviction. We have touched and handled the Word of Life, the experience of St. John, and, Woe is me if I preach not the Gospel, the self-realization of St. Paul, are the necessity of the Christian prophet.

The whole Church is the messenger of God for the salvation of mankind. The Church exists for the propagation of the Gospel, and the commission of Christ was given to the body in its integrity. The existence of the Church affirms certain historic truths, and witnesses to certain Divine powers. Forms of liturgy and styles of architecture saliently tell something of the Incarnation. And as Abraham was called that all the generations of the earth might be blessed so the Church was formed for the world, and every Christian is under the obligation of service that the salvation of all men may be set forward. The commission given to the whole Church is exercised by the Christian ministry, but there is no reason to assume that the ministry has this commission for itself apart from the Church. And still less is there any ground for suggesting that any separate apostolic line is traceable in the successors of a particular Apostle. Such a phrase as " St. Peter and his successors " indicates a confusion of ideas; the apostolate is a function in the Church and the whole Church is responsible for the fulfilment of that function.

In the episcopate and the ministerial priesthood we have the ordinary expression and fulfilment of this function, but the work of converting the world is now being attempted very inadequately. And. the failure of the Church in this matter is chiefly due to the lay-people. Many cavil readily and protest that the clergy are exclusive in their ministry, but the remedy is not far to seek. The Christian life is the necessary support of the Christian doctrine. In the Church the lay-people greatly preponderate and the weakness of Christianity is not to be found so much in defective statement from the pulpit as in lack of corresponding support in the ordinary lives of the people. Conversion is produced more by infection than by dialectic, and the whole Christian body must be engaged in the leavening of mankind. Apparently there are many to-day who are ready to claim some of the advantages of Christianity without acknowledging the obligations of fellowship and

membership in the Church. Their attitude towards
Creed and Sacrament is that of scepticism; their discipleship is of no more practical value than that of
Pontius Pilate, who was convinced of the innocence of
Christ and desired earnestly to save Him from death
but was overborne by public clamour. Fidelity to membership is the great necessity of these times; a man
definitely heretical deserves the name of Christian better
than the general sceptic. And general scepticism with
no appreciation of the existence, not to say supreme
importance, of spiritual truth commonly wears the
mask of charity and broadmindedness.

But if Christ gave His commission to His Church
He also appointed the constitution for His society.
He publicly announced to the whole body of His dis-
ciples the appointment of certain Apostles.

The twelve Apostles were chosen as witnesses and
not as authors; St. Peter making his defence before the
council said, "We cannot but speak the things which
we have seen and heard," and again on another occasion,
" We are His witnesses of these things, and so is also
the Holy Ghost Whom God hath given to them that
obey Him ". It is evident that our Lord chose His
Apostles with this purpose; they were not such men as
might be selected for a great enterprise demanding
initiative. They were eminently simple, direct, sober,
sincere; their qualities were rather fidelity and tenacity
than originality or subtlety. The people amongst whom
our Lord moved in His earthly ministry were representative of those qualities of the mental soul which offer
the greatest resistance to religious thought. The Greek
temper of scepticism and the Roman habit of materialism were there together with that hardened incredulity
of the Jews which was the outcome of centuries of in-

tense religious feeling and defeated national hope.   Such
a soil is of all the least promising for a spiritual harvest,
but there the Sower went forth to sow.   As on Carmel
the fire of the Lord fell upon the thrice drenched sacri-
fice and licked up the water that was in the trench, so
the Gospel was given first to a people whose conditions
seemed to make its acceptance impossible.   The Twelve
were chosen not to commend the faith with arguments
and learning but to support the facts with insistent
testimony.   And the direction of St. Paul in restraint
of the preaching of women was not only to protect the
modesty of Christian womanhood but also to defend
Christianity from emotionalism which would imperil
the tradition of calm narrative and plain record.

And the chosen Twelve were trained by the Master for
their work.   They were restrained and corrected and
disciplined into self-distrust; they were brought by personal experience to know their Master as the Son of
God.   They were allowed rather than encouraged to
make the profession of their faith; they were taught to
rely upon direct gifts of the Holy Spirit.   And their
ministry as recorded in the book of the Acts bore this
relation to the work of Jesus Christ; they set Him before their hearers, they placarded as it were His Crucifixion and bore witness to His Resurrection.   This was
the necessity of the first age of Christianity, but presently apostles went beyond the limits of Israel and
carried the Gospel to men who had no knowledge of
prophecy and no discipline of moral law.   Of necessity
the Christian prophet used then an extended ministry,
and all the significance of the old terms seer and prophet revived with greater value.   The prophet to-day
with the full reception of the great truths of the Incarnation and the Atonement fills the office of moral and

spiritual leadership; he must be eyes and lips for many that cannot see or speak.

The study of the Old Testament Scriptures shows that the prophet must have two qualifications for his work. First he must speak boldly as one that shall answer to His Master whether people hear or forbear. In the old dispensation the prophets usually came in from without; they were raised up in one place to carry their message to another. Jonah to Nineveh, Amos to Bethel, the man of Judah to Samaria are illustrations of this Divine method. This gave a certain vantage ground to the preacher; he spoke with freedom as he stood aloof and detached. He was in no danger of social compromise. The preaching of the Son of God Himself was ineffective in His own country where people said, "Is not this the carpenter's Son? Is not His Mother called Mary? Are not His brethren and His sisters here with us?" And the preacher from without can take the measure of things more accurately than they can who grow up within the system social or religious. It does not necessarily imply dishonesty or cowardice, but we are all quick to see the faults of a state or society that differs greatly from our own.

And secondly, the prophet must have a simple and direct intuition or vision of the unseen. He must be demonized by the truth that he has to announce. He must know himself as the voice of truth, the mouthpiece of God. This was the temper of the old prophets, "Jehovah hath spoken, who can but prophesy?" And this was the calling of St. John the Baptist: "I am the voice of one crying in the wilderness". It is the sick hurry of our times that has reduced everything to disproportioned and confused littleness. Behind the ministry of the old prophets was the sense of God's sublimity and

lofty majesty.   The desert was the school of Moses and
Elijah and Amos and St. John Baptist.   As in 2 Esdras
IX. v. 26—" I went my way into the field and there I sat
among the flowers and did eat of the herbs of the field
and the meat of the same satisfied me.   After seven
days I sat upon the grass, and my heart was vexed
within me like as before : and I opened my mouth and
began to talk before the Most High and said, O Lord,
Thou that shewest Thyself unto us, Thou wast shewed
unto our fathers in the wilderness, in a place where no
man treadeth, in a barren place."   One of our modern
writers has told us that all the great religions have
been born in places of sparse population, and have become popularized when carried into towns and cities.
And we still need the moral setting afforded by the
desert life, the sense of the infinite and the sternness of
nature.   We shall escape from the neurotic and hysterical best by great solitudes and silences.   Personal
religion at its root must have some personal conception
of God, and we need to be careful to identify the God of
grace with the God of nature, and to know that the
sacraments are related to the planets.   The first confession of the Nicene Creed may gain as much from
our holidays as from our libraries.   The study of such
sciences as astronomy and geology and botany is of
the utmost value to the preacher who would speak in
the name of " the dear God Who loveth us and made
and loveth all ".

And further such experience and such study inspires
a right temper of frugality and simplicity of life.   This
is one of the great needs of this age.   The common
craze for pleasure and self-enjoyment is a most frequent cause of moral failure amongst our people.   The
haste to be rich that one may enjoy all that riches

command is a prolific cause of irreligion ; and fraud, embezzlement, bankruptcy and suicide come in this train. The corrective of this widespread social disease must begin with those who "scorn delights and live laborious days". Plain living and high thinking still go together, and personal discipline is the first contribution to the health of the whole body of the redeemed. The social life of the clergy, often innocent and delightful as a merely social existence, is apt to muffle their message and to rob their exhortations of penetrative force.

Our Church suffers great disadvantages from the settled conditions of the parochial clergy ; we need a supplement of men constantly moving through the dioceses in wider fields of ministry. We might readily claim for ourselves all the advantages of the circuit system of the Wesleyans without its disadvantages. The theory of the payment of our clergy is not that their labours are sufficiently remunerated from their benefices, but that they are maintained by the Church whilst they work for the Church. Any young priest between 25 and 30 years of age would find ample maintenance if he would offer himself to his bishop to work without remuneration or reward. And every young priest ought to give at least three years to missionary work at home or abroad. If we had in every diocese a group of fifteen or twenty men who had passed through the parochial apprenticeship of two years following ordination, and had then given themselves to diocesan ministries for a definite term, the Church would be enormously helped and strengthened. These young priests moving under the direction of a warden appointed by the bishop would carry a living and kindling influence into every corner of the diocese, would encourage and stimulate the older clergy in lonely cures, and revive the prophetic function

of the Church.   They would learn whilst they taught.
They would acquire flexibility of method, they would
gain experience of varying parishes, they would discover
what brotherhood means, they would find how to adapt
themselves readily to environment, they would get a
sense of proportion which would rid them of partisanship in theology and ecclesiastical affairs.   And later in
life they would know that this was their greater university training, their experience as sons of the prophets.
Dupanloup, the great Bishop of Orleans, commanded his
preachers to walk much in mountainous regions that
they might accustom themselves to physical fatigue and
rustic simplicity ; he knew how greatly such conditions
would develop moral strength and personal directness.

The preacher who comes in from without has the advantage of approaching the soul in an unusual manner.
The ordinary and familiar way loses its power.   To get
at the soul effectively it is necessary first to strip off the
wrappings of convention and custom, and next to raise
the moral temperature.   The stranger can do this more
easily and naturally than the ordinary pastor with whom
the people are familiar.   The instinct of one who listens
often to the same phrases uttered in the same tones is
to harden oneself to the appeal, but an unfamiliar voice
strikes in at a new angle and arrests attention and may
compel thought.   The advantage of this opportunity
must not be squandered ; too soon the freshness of
voice and manner will have passed away, and such opportunities cannot be created without limit.   In using
this prophetic ministry there is need of great self-restraint ; unmeasured declamation, over-emphasis or
disproportion in exhortation, apparent want of self-
control or of judgment will vitiate and invalidate the

most earnest utterance.   The spirit of the prophet must
be subject to the prophet.   In teaching it must be
always remembered that the learner already knows
something and that the teacher has to build up towards
completeness the knowledge already existing in part ;
in the same way the prophet has to encourage and reinforce a conscience already in possession.   He mistakes
his work if he supposes that he has to create or lend a
conscience ; he must rather aim at claiming an audience
within for the voice that has been drowned by the
clamour of self-interest or the chatter of trivialities.
One begins with the recognition that God has not left
Himself without a witness within man, and one associ-
ates the external ministry with the internal mission of
the Holy Spirit.   It is necessary at the same time to
apply to human lives the corrective of an absolute
standard by which men may measure themselves.
Comparing themselves with themselves they are not
wise, and they must be brought to know the true ideal
and the true purpose of human life.   This means that
sympathy and severity are needed in the prophetic ministry, a sympathy that notes gladly all the good that
exists in humanity and a severity that makes unhesitating demands upon every man.   We are charged with
" warning everyman and teaching everyman," and this
is the necessary order, just as the covenant of law preceded the revelation of Divine love ; negative precept
is given for the restraint of our fallen nature before we
can become vessels for the Divine indwelling.   The
law was for the pruning of our nature that it might
later bring forth the fruits of the Spirit.   " Warning
everyman," suggests the putting away of illusions and
sophistries which cheat man of his knowledge and serve
in place of religious truth ; we must help men to know

the worthlessness of Satan's spurious currency and then they may come to value God's golden truth.

The prophets of the old covenant enforced by their ministry the obligations of the law. They gave the support of personal directness to the code which might readily become evaded by equivocation and social custom. The word of God was constantly made of none effect by man's tradition, and the irregularity of the prophets served to break tradition and maintain the living claim of the law. The covenant of law shaped the national character of the Hebrew people. In every close population men instinctively claim for themselves some compensations for the loss of the pleasures of nature; art and drama pitifully attempt to afford to towns-people something in place of the more wholesome joys of moor and forest and stream and mountain. And these diversions of theatre and picture gallery bring artificiality into human character. The decalogue straitly forbade art and drama, and under its Divine restraints the people became serious and corporately conscious of national life, moving under the guidance of the hand of God. Seriousness is the sense of continuity and causality; it stands in contrast to the fitful and sporadic and accidental. Seriousness is the necessary temper for all who would learn of God; it is the mind of Moses as he reflects: " Before the mountains were brought forth or ever the earth and the world were made, Thou art God from everlasting, and world without end. A thousand years in Thy sight are but as yesterday. We bring our years to an end as it were a tale that is told. So teach us to number our days that we may apply our hearts unto wisdom."

The prophets applied the law to the case, and brought it down from the general to the particular, to the moral

need of the age.   Christ Himself referred to the ministry
of law and prophets as a necessary preparation for the
coming of the Word of God into the world.   In speaking
of souls for whom a special and phenomenal ministry
was prayed He declared, "If they hear not Moses and
the prophets, neither will they be persuaded though one
rose from the dead".   The Gospel of the Resurrection
can be most readily received by those in whom the law
and the prophets have wrought a moral preparedness of
discipline and seriousness.   Self-indulgence and lack of
moral earnestness render the soul incapable of seeing
the light.   Spiritual truth is the prize given to moral
disposition.   The decay of parental discipline in our
times is one of the most serious losses that our national
character has suffered.   The old position of the father
in the home, authoritative and almost magisterial, has
been replaced by an attitude of capricious fondness
which has in it no suggestion of authority or discipline.
It is in the homely and closely personal relationships of
parents and children, and of husbands and wives
that are generated self-sacrifice and forethought, and
through these relationships the accumulated qualities
pass from generation to generation.   The capacity for
spiritual knowledge is wanting in persons who have
grown up in unrestraint and animal indulgence.   This
condition of sterility of soul is seen in its plainest expression in the hotel-bred people of American cities.

The social conditions most conducive to the promotion of personal religion are those which supply a constant and certain foundation of order together with some
elements of personal variability; as in nature one may
remark fixed laws of gravitation and evaporation with
unforeseen changes of wind and weather.   The barrack
system for orphans as gravely fails to form character

as the life of a travelling tinker's family.   Regularity
with variability is the best aid to the formation of character and a well-ordered home is most likely to produce
this state.   It is remarkable that the excesses of criminal
violence are found amongst persons of no home life.
The leaders of the French Revolution, for example, were
unmarried men of the educated and professional classes.
Dean Colet of St. Paul's, in founding his great school,
committed it to the care of married citizens of London.
Erasmus writes, "When some one asked him why, he
answered that though there were always risks in human
affairs yet these were the men in whom he had always
found least dishonesty".   It must be remembered that
disposition has to be cultivated and developed if conviction is to prove a living force in the direction of conduct and the formation of character.   The change of
moral climate or feeling will often suffice without the
addition of a single argument to make at once credible
that which before seemed impossible.   Probably at the
present day more needs to be done in the way of forming
the personal disposition than in the matter of construct-
ing arguments.   The Christian faith has through nine-
teen centuries verified itself in human experience : and
the surest grounds of personal confidence in Christ are
those which are experimentally ascertained.

As in the old covenant the work of the prophet was
chiefly the emphasis of some particularly relevant part
of the law so in the new covenant the preacher has to
apply the Gospel to life.   For this work he needs to
know life and not only theology.   St. John the Baptist
knew how to advise town-dwellers though he himself
lived his life in the wilderness.   He learned from the
people themselves, as they came out in multitudes con-
fessing their sins.   And St. Paul learned as he taught,

and taught as he learned, an Apostle and a tent-maker with his fellow-craftsmen in Corinth. The course of instruction received by ordination candidates to-day might be enlarged to good effect if three months in the year were spent upon the road or in some manual employment; and the sermons of our preachers would gain freshness and cogency if preachers themselves had the training of St. John Baptist in hearing the self-accusations of their people.

Two missions were preached in a great parish church in the north of England with an interval of ten years, one of these by the most fluent preacher of his day, and the other by one who halted and hesitated and knew no graces of diction. The former dealt with no individual soul and left no traceable result. The other found his public ministry embarrassed by the eagerness of persons under conscious burden of sin; the results of this mission were incalculable. One of the two knew rhetoric and the other knew humanity, and that made all the difference. He that would deal with men effectively must know what is in man. He must reckon with the worst and expect the best of which our nature is capable. St. John Chrysostom writes: "We speak of great truths and live for great destinies"; and the Christian prophet must never lose hope or allow himself to inspire despair in his hearers. There are some political speakers who appeal to what is basest and meanest in the human heart, and they may by their cleverness and lack of principle carry their audiences with them for a time. But a man who has been moved by such appeals instinctively resents the means employed to reach him, and despises the politician who has affected him. The great orators, the best teachers and leaders of men, have addressed themselves to the generous sentiments

4

and the noble impulses of their hearers; and under their spell men have found themselves capable of being far better than they had imagined possible.

We have to inspire men not only with desire but with hope for better things; we have to move them to believe that they are capable of becoming that which we have taught them to admire. And in our ministry a certain severity holds as important a place as this confidence in humanity. The false prophet betrays himself by his acquiescence, in his assent to compromise, his willingness to accept terms, his accommodation to local conditions. It is impossible for us as teachers to command the respect of men if we manifestly condone what their own consciences condemn. St. Paul exhorted the elders of Ephesus to take care of the flock which God had purchased with His Own Blood; the Atonement shows us at once the preciousness of man and the heinousness of sin. The position of a crucifix over against the pulpit in continental churches, where the glance of the preacher easily lights upon it, may serve this purpose—to tell the worth of man and point the horror of sin. And in our own land some of our northern bishops in the seventeenth century ordered painted texts to be placed upon the walls of the churches, with one invariable text over against the pulpit, " Cry aloud, spare not, lift up thy voice like a trumpet and show My people their transgression, and the house of Jacob their sins ". The effect that the preacher should desire to produce in the hearts of the people is this: men must be brought to know themselves as they are, to feel conviction of sin, to realize what they may become, to have the hope of personal salvation. The prophetic ministry makes the question of religion urgently personal, and brings it home with direct purpose. As

Nathan first evoked the indignation of David against wrong-doing and then directed the force of that indignation against the king himself, "Thou art the man," so must the preacher to-day marshal what is best in human nature against all that is unworthy and base, and help men to see themselves as they are, with a quenchless hope also that they may become something worthy of the love of God that redeems us.

4 *

CHAPTER IV.

HEARING THE WORD.

IN the exercise of the ministry of the Word we have to consider the right direction of the appeal. To what in man must we address ourselves? It has been usual sometimes to portray the horrors of endless retribution, the pains of the damned, and the hopelessness of the lost. Converts have been made by such terrifying methods, but it is difficult to believe that such converts were wholesomely brought under the guidance of the Spirit. The inducements of fear are not likely to promote a love of God and a great temper of self-humbling. And later that method of terror has given place to the method of barter, which offers the choice of heaven as a prize and reward to those who are willing to accept membership in some religious body on earth. The appeal in this case is to selfishness and self-love; as a moral quality this is no higher than the former motive of fear. The spiritual life is for itself and in itself the true life of man without regard to possibilities or consequences of heaven or hell. Whilst it is impossible to overstate the importance of our knowing that the life of Christ already begun in us is the life of the world to come, yet too great an emphasis may easily be laid upon the consideration of our fortune hereafter. It is evident that our Lord would not draw into discipleship any persons on the prospect of gain or reward. He put before men the plainest warning when they offered themselves as followers: the Son of Man hath not where to lay His Head, and the servant must be as His Master. He taught that none were capable of heaven till they became indifferent to earth, that as He had come forth as a servant to seek man, so man should find Him through ways of lowliness and self-denial.

If then we must not weight our appeal or argument with threats or bribes which touch directly human nature, how shall we move our hearers? It is the will in man that has made revolt against God and consequent confusion within; and it is through the will, recovered into loyalty, that man must be remade. But the will is not reached directly or nakedly; it must be approached through conviction and persuasion. My will is not mine unless the spring of its action lies within me, and I am something less than a man if my will merely registers the decision of another. The preacher has to deal with a complexity of qualities lying deeper than the will itself; the will roots back into all that makes up to the total of character. It is clear that a mathematical demonstration cannot effect a moral change, and that no statement of spiritual truth, however compendious and logical, can compel universal conversion. The will has two great assessors, knowledge and feeling. It is necessary to approach the will by informing the knowledge and moving the feeling. But these subdivide again and the contents of knowledge are not all the simple ascertainments of our perceptive senses, equally clear, equally cogent, and equally important; nor is feeling a mere quantity, more or less in extent or volume. The Christian prophet has to reach the will through conviction. He must convince through the understanding and the affections. And these are two considerable parts of our problem : how to enlighten the understanding, and how to promote the disposition.

Undue haste is as fatal in this work as false motives are to the result. Let it be remembered that what is sought as the final object is such a redirection of the human will as must, in the course of long years of patience, form a new character, a spiritual being, the fruit of the Passion of Christ Jesus. The redirected human will is to be the core of this new creation, and humanly speaking the creative force of the new manhood. We have not to lightly heal the wound of our people ; we have to retrace the path by which man has wandered from God that Christ may see of the travail of His Soul and be satisfied. And in many cases, before this reconstruction of character can make much progress, the will itself needs to be freed and strengthened. For it is a danger of close populations that people are apt to will less, and to act without reflection upon contagion. In sparse populations the sense of personal responsibility is more constant, but with the enlargement of society comes the enthralment of the person. It has been rightly said, Man first makes the State and then the State makes man. The creature of the State is not comparable with the author of the constitution. And the adherent who is brought in by a sweeping movement is rarely of a quality that promises spiritual progress. The freedom of the will is the spring of character. The existence of free will is sometimes denied as being theoretically untenable and inconsistent with analysis. But all experience goes to affirm that free will exists, and that every volition moves to form character. As Dr. Johnson said: " The arguments are on one side and experience on the other; the freedom of the will is a matter of primary consciousness ". It is important that we affirm this, and strive to promote the temper of resoluteness and decisiveness in life. Christianity in the periods of its strongest advance has laid great emphasis upon the will and its sacredness. And the Greek fathers exalt self-determination; the same line is taken by the Alexandrian school. And Tertullian writes that the freedom of the will is the unmistakable sign and symbol of the royalty of man. As the future hegemony of Europe will inevitably fall to the nation that resists the tendency to race suicide, so the spiritual conquest of the world will be made by that religion which best generates the will force of its disciples. In every homogeneous group of persons the tendency is to lower the force of will, and increase the intensity of feeling. An impassioned mob is inhuman and may become demoniacal; it acts upon suggestion without reflection and exults in outrage and violence.

In the mind of the crowd there is little reason or reflection, and consequently a leader who can arouse feeling is himself its mind so far as purpose is concerned. The crowd so dominated has an excess of emotion and sensation and a corresponding lack of reason and deliberate intention. And where the mob or crowd is in looser form, the population of a parish or of a township, the same mental and moral condition exists though in less marked degree.

It is well to teach people to be alert to resist what is called public opinion, and further to be resolute always to give a lead to others in moments of indecision. A man who has already made up his mind can, if he is alert, commit the great majority of his friends to the same conclusions as himself. He will effect this best when he acts without apparent effort or intention. It is proverbial that the greatest sinners transformed have become the greatest saints; this is only another way of saying that a strong personality counts for much on any course that it takes. And we must cultivate the will, with a realization that willessness is in these days a more common danger than wilfulness.

The will acts upon knowledge and feeling; or it may be said with St. Thomas Aquinas, Man is determined by a combination of reason and appetite. The appeal of the Christian ministry must satisfy both; revealed truth is not contrary to reason, and Christ lifted up draws the hearts of all men. Ordinarily men do not readily believe specious statements which seem to be accommodations, but they are attracted by truth when it is plainly uncompromising. We have not to offer sophistries to the world, or to lure men to some profession of religion by minimizing its claim or veiling its severity. If ever there were any wisdom in that method there is none to-day, for all men instinctively know the common need of strong correctives and moral tonics in modern life, and Christianity alone can meet this need. The gospels of good nature and thrift and sociability, the vain puerilities of half our modern religious movements, are wearing out the patience of people whose fathers knew at least the seriousness of Christianity. The Old Testament conception of God is necessary to the doctrine of the Incarnation, and the

Puritan austerity was defective only in its lack of proportion. If any one element of character is to stand alone, severity is not so grave a misrepresentation of Christianity as sentimentality or indulgence.

The preacher has no warrant for making his message as the " very lovely song of one that hath a pleasant voice and can play well on an instrument "; the hearer must find the note of austerity and the standard of holiness in the ministry that is to hold him with greater spell and power than his own instincts and self-interests. And it must not be forgotten that the tone or note of the messenger effects much for good or ill without regard to the contents of the message. The hearer does not wait to consider the credibility or acceptability of your conclusions, but is predisposed or prejudiced from the beginning. Attention must be won and the will-to-believe must be engaged, that presently the will to live anew may be formed and strengthened. The will-to-believe is the necessary ignition upon which the life inspired by grace follows. We cannot then neglect the will whilst we inform the mind or appeal to the heart. Whilst psychologically we follow that order for convenience in shaping our ministry, in practice the three, reason, affection, and will are involved.

The mind is enriched by two means, perception and reflection; by perception it acquires and by reflection it utilizes and increases its stores. But since 1886 we have been aware of the subliminal consciousness, that larger mind vested with memory and thought and feeling, and effective to originate impulses and suggestions. This subliminal mind, as Mr. Myers named it, collects without effort and without notice unmeasured material that passes unchallenged into the mental soul. With this secondary consciousness the preacher must reckon, for he has to do with complete man and not merely with an array of measured qualities.

Our ordinary predispositions are doubtless in large measure derived from the subliminal mind, and the instinctive direction of conduct without volition is in this domain. It is usual to attribute too much in the way of the formation of character to environment, but so far as environment counts it is almost wholly through the subconscious. And this must be our principal purpose in arranging the form and manner of religious observations for young people. It is not only that they may be provoked to ask " What mean ye by this service ? " The regularity and frequency of an act will make it less probable that any question will be asked ; but these conditions of regularity and frequency may tell through the subconscious, and ultimately do more than prompt a question that may be answered verbally.

The principal forces at the summons of the preacher are already within man ; as when St. Paul moved a dishonest official by reasoning of righteousness, temperance, and judgment. The claim of God speaks with a native accent to the soul of man, and the preacher may confidently rely upon much in man which is not consciously held or recognized. In the experience of such converts as St. Augustine the divided will, in the process of unification through disturbance, is the outcome of the subconscious breaking up into the conscious. It cannot be assumed that the subconscious is a higher element of our mental constitution than the conscious, but the awakening of the latent faculties of the subconscious, and the combination of these with the well-recognized forces and possessions of the conscious, make a singular and immediate fertility both of reason and affection.

There is no influence that touches ordinary lives more
deeply than the religious; and consequently none that
takes so greatly the risk of mental disturbance or un-
balance. It has been observed by some writers like Dr.
Starbuck that conversions of a certain kind are invariably to be found within that brief zone which marks the
attainment of puberty in either sex. But it must be
noted that this period is itself one of intense emotional
disturbance and of exalted sensitiveness. And therefore
whatever object is presented to the mind of one in such
unsettled conditions is likely to be seen in strange disproportion and exaggeration. Plainly the utmost care
must be taken when one has to deal with young people
in an emotional state; hysteria will sometimes si-
mulate devotion, and the mind may lose its balance
altogether under the strain of excitement.

It cannot be fairly charged against religion that it produces insanity; but it may be incidentally noted that the
appeal of the preacher is to the largest contents of our
mental constitution, and that the aim of the preacher is
to deal with all the factors, and settle the personal character on its true basis. If then the preacher wishes to
address his audience inclusively he must not content
himself with a narrative statement of revealed truth;
this might be offered to the perceptions alone. He must
reckon with the whole mental soul of his hearers, and
stimulate also reflection. And he must do this in such
a manner as to predispose to belief those who hear.
Christianity stands firmly upon historical foundations;
the Creed consists largely of records of events. But the
acceptance of these statements is not compulsory, for it
is evidently possible to reject and deny them. Religious
belief is more than mental acquiescence; as it must
move to action it contains in itself the moral as well as

the mental element.   And the temper consistent with a right relationship with God is the necessary climate for the believing soul.   A butterfly taken alive from a Swiss valley to a level above the snow line becomes frozen and crystallized and may be blown to dust by a breath, but if it be taken without fraction back to the valley and into the sunshine it flies lightly away.   The Word must be mixed with faith in them that hear it, and from the first note there must be the temper of faith induced by suggestion and personal infection.   The manner purely forensic or professional or academical is fatally impossible for the ministry of conversion.   St. Paul addressing Greeks makes his appeal to the teachings of nature and throws his argument upon the moral sense of his hearers, " I speak as to wise men, judge ye what I say ".   The intellect alone could not discover God, though reason must assent to His claim upon man as an intellectual being.

The Latin maxim runs, " We speak that we may persuade, and persuade that we may move ".   The Word is given to men that they may find it a power unto salvation. In fact we only hold as much truth as holds us ; and fidelity to truth is the condition of our retaining the knowledge of truth.   The preacher must find the proofs of his orthodoxy in the demeanour of his people, their concern in missionary work and social righteousness. Spiritual knowledge can never be merely acquisition ; it must be of necessity inspiration.   This brings us to the question of motive.   Of all the considerations that pass in succession before our people upon which do they act generally ?   It is readily assumed that the religious motive is usually high and generous.   But inquiry will show that few people are sufficiently free and detached to choose deliberately ideals in life.   And secondary considerations or, as they may appear to be, accidental circumstances often determine the choice even at the great crises of life. More often than we suppose people are moved by provocation rather than by attraction. And that because the attracting influences are sedative and leave the soul unmoved and complaisant, whilst by provocation one may be compelled to question one's security. But in any case, whilst we all affirm that the Christian life depends upon the individual will, yet we accept in practice a state of things entirely at variance with this acknowledgment.

It is impossible to believe that the settled state of membership in the various religious denominations in this country can be satisfactorily explained in any other way than this; personal selection and deliberate choice are rare in matters of religion. And we must note with regret that the vigorous and wilful temper of the ancestor who broke from the Church has left no trace of self-direction in his acquiescent descendant. It needs to be taught with insistence that every one is severally responsible for his religious beliefs. To profess oneself a member of any particular body on the ground that one's parents were in that body is to set oneself down an ancestor worshipper. Christ claimed for Himself the immediate obedience of every Christian; He warned men to reckon none upon earth father or author of their faith. The acceptance of membership in a religious society as a part of our social condition or status is the reduction of religion to a petty and accidental quality of family life.

These truths must be affirmed with all plainness. If it be answered that they imperil our own position, and threaten the reduction of our own membership by the loss of the great company of persons who profess themselves Church-people solely on the ground that their parents made the same profession, we have a sufficient reply to that demurrer. The number of adherents that the Church owes to this cause is a weakness not a strength to her spiritual character. It is conceivable that the Church would become infinitely stronger as a force to fight social evil and as an instrument to convert the world if she lost two-thirds of her present nominal members. When God chose Gideon as the leader of the army through whom He would deliver Israel from Midian, He appointed two winnowing processes to sift out the warriors from the rabble. First He bade Gideon send away the irresolute and the willess, and of 32,000 all but 10,000 returned home. Then He commanded Gideon to bring the 10,000 to the water, and to dismiss as worthless all who drank with unrestraint and filled themselves with water: and with this test of discipline He reduced the 10,000 to 300. The 300 resolute and restrained went out with the blessing of God and came back victorious. To-day the Church is weak because a great mass of Church members are accidentally with us, without individual decision and without personal discipline. It may of course follow rightly that the children have the same religious convictions as their parents; but this legitimate succession would be the result of careful home training and doctrinal teaching. Parents are too often apparently careless of the duty of teaching religion to their children, and accept with little interest the diversion of their nearest relations to various beliefs and denials. Probably the Sunday School system, which as a means of teaching religion to children has been largely over-rated, is responsible not only for the loss of public catechizing but also for the neglect of home instruction in the truths of Christianity.

But it is necessary to say that with all the defects of casual or merely customary attendance at Church it sometimes happens that true membership and real devotion begin from this habit. Though familiarity usually deadens the sense of attention yet the shaft may sometimes get home through the joints of the harness, and personal religion does sometimes, if rarely, arise out of merely hereditary custom in Church going. The occasions of conversion amongst men who have been marched to a Church parade are less rare; for though such an attendance at service may seem to be on a lower ground than that of family custom, the individual is less hardened to the appeal of the Gospel.

We speak that we may persuade, and we persuade that we may move. It is to be desired, then, that those who hear should have a disposition to receive the Word. And the manner of the preacher in large measure determines the disposition of the hearer. It is possible to harden hesitation into scepticism, or to stiffen doubt into denial, or to excite instinctive distrust, or to provoke counter considerations. If the preacher finds it necessary to deal with controversial questions on any occasion, he is under obligation to state the case of the adversary as justly and strongly as possible. If he fails to do this he will create a suspicion of bad faith or ignorance in the minds of his hearers, and will lose their sympathy. But if when he has stated the case fully he evidently fails to answer it completely he will have given away the argument. It is necessary to retain the confidence of the hearers by evident sincerity and honesty, and to keep them under persuasion by doing justice to their need of conviction. The preacher must encourage the will-to-believe by such use of the imagination of his people as will form in them a great admira-

tion for virtue and spiritual gifts. It has been usual to
attribute conversion invariably in its beginning to a
profound sense of sin, but it would be a poor and partial
record of Christianity which left out of account the
many who have come like Synesius to find in Christianity the perfect philosophy and to claim it as the
sacred fire. Probably as we return from the Latin and
legalist conceptions of Christianity to the synthetic
teachings of the Alexandrian school we shall come to
regard the John Bunyan type of conversion as a lower
and rarer method of grace than that of Pattison or
Keble. The attraction of that wisdom of God which has
constituted the services of angels and men in a wonderful order will bring more disciples into grace than the
realization of a disordered self under a burden of guilt.

Happily one of the results which modern science has
given us in a larger knowledge of the natural universe is the sense of harmonious inter-relationship of
every part with the whole. And the pressure of that
recognition is compelling even the scientist to seek for
his place in the discipleship. Sir Oliver Lodge in his
endeavours to construct a religious way by the light of
science acknowledges that he has found this need, and
must be restless till he rests in God. We may be confident that since all existence other than God is the out-
speech of God's will everything that exists needs all
else for its own completeness ; and man, knowing himself, must know his need of that One towards Whom his
best moves. It has been thought that the spiritual sense
is limited to persons comparatively few, but this is not
consistent with the Christian Gospel. If we have found
that our method has apparently availed for few let us
reconsider our method. To determine beforehand that
all men approaching God must take a certain way of

emotion and relief is to limit salvation to a certain class
of persons. Christianity in the first ages discovered and
proclaimed the universality of those faculties in man
which enable the soul to know itself in the presence of
God and to live in an immediate relationship with God.

The preacher recognizing this must encourage and
cultivate the temper of reverence and mystery in his
hearers; for mystery is the acknowledgment of God's
transcendent greatness, that He is not altogether such
an one as self. The use of a language in the pulpit
that does not befit the dignity and sacredness of our
theme is condemnable on practical grounds; it hinders
spiritual reception by destroying the right disposition to
receive. It has been wisely said that "the furniture of
the Church, the subdued light, twin candles in the sanc-
tuary, the restrained and quiet harmonies of organ and
choir, all conduce to form what is called the atmosphere,"
and to engage the teachable and impressionable attention of the people. Mr. Spurgeon in other terms taught
the same prudence; that however we may rely upon the
word spoken, we must also reckon with the physiological
and psychological condition of those who hear.

Reason, affection, and will are not separable or
measurable in course of development or action; they
interpenetrate one another. The will-to-believe may
be induced by something of the affections aroused, as,
for instance, an admiration of virtue; and the will-to-
believe itself predisposes reason to assent, and excites
kindly interpretation. Assent and kindly interpretation
themselves move the will to definite decisions and the
life of discipleship follows. But then further this life itself is the formation and development of the Christian
character, and the Christian character is a prepared vessel
for the reception of spiritual truth. So it comes about

that truth accepted and occupied makes a further capacity to hear, to discern, to retain, and to appropriate Divine knowledge. It is necessary to observe that the character so formed under the inspiration of revealed truth is not the merely moral but the spiritual character. The fruits of the Spirit are not thrift, sobriety, cleanliness, prudence; these are qualities of character, good or indifferent, which are put on externally and have their reward in this life. The Christian character may contain such qualities in some form, but only incidentally; it is primarily the spiritual creation. The preacher is not only wasting time when he is attempting to force improvements of the personal and social character, he is hopelessly confusing the issue and sterilizing the rudimentary sense of the spiritual amongst his people. The Hebrews as they left Egypt were a servile race, coarse in gluttony and instinctively given to idolatry; the Divine tutelage of this people began with abstract lessons of pure monotheism. The teaching concerning Jehovah, One, Absolute, All-holy, preceded the prohibitions of murder, and lust, and rapine. And the Christian character is the expression in human nature of revealed truth made known in Christ, and received by the heart of faith.

The spiritual is greater than the moral as the son is greater in the house than the servant; the moral man is the servant of God, the spiritual man is God's own son. And the spiritual life must gradually clothe itself in moral habitudes. The Christian preacher must not only warn himself that the moral is rather the foliage than the fruit; he must note where Christian morality differs from ethics of heathenism or of modern sociologists. The moralist who becomes the spiritual man shifts his centre from self to God and enlarges his circumference immeasurably. He keeps no longer a ledger account with mankind of debt and credit; his new nature is to grow up into Christ in all things, and to bear the burdens of others. This distinction works out with such inevitableness that every separate quality of either moralist or Christian is unmistakably typical. And one might almost add that a quality which appears to be virtue in the spiritual man as, for instance, thrift, has in the ethical man almost the deformity of vice. For the temper of origin tones the whole development of a human quality, whether it be self-regard or self-sacrifice.

It is to the ultimate character complete in Christ that the preacher must address himself from the first word. The healing of the man of Decapolis who had an impediment in his speech, illustrates for us the process of conversion. Through the arrested attention and kindled expectation of the man, Christ urgent and intimate gave new powers to dull and incoherent faculties. So the Christian preacher must bring the human soul under the influence of the Spirit, must lift the regard heavenward, and open the avenues between the heart and God that He may be heard and praised. Our ministry must mediate between God and the soul; it must be transparent of the light and significant of the power of God. And whilst it is clear that the offer must be made to all men the preacher should beware lest a desire for large numbers divert him from the less attractive work of ministering to the spiritual. Of the preacher about to ascend the pulpit we may ask, first, To what in man will you address yourself? second, What motive do you propose to engage in your hearers? and third, What is the ultimate object of your appeal? And the ministry will gain in effectiveness when those three questions can be definitely answered.

5 *

The preacher must address himself to the spiritual man existent potentially in every soul; he must move his hearers to desire to take Divine wisdom as a bride, and to live in conformity with the Will of God; he must direct all his ministry to the one purpose, to present every man finally perfect in Christ.

CHAPTER V.

THE WORD RECEIVED.

Necessary Moral Affinity—Effect of Common Influences—Sympathetic Understanding—Sincerity and Teachableness—Believing in Christ —The Incarnation—The Whole Truth—The Gospel for all People— The Mind of the Church—Tradition and Growth—New Testament Terms—Disciples of Christ—The Brethren in Christ—The Saints of God—High Spiritual Standards—The Faithful in Christ Jesus—The Vision of the Unseen—The Harmony of all Things in Christ—The Heathen in God's Temple—False Attractions—The Claim of Duty.

ST. PAUL, in writing to St. Timothy, notes that God was proclaimed unto the nations and believed on in the world; the reception of Divine truth is necessary if it is to be effective. In every soul there is capacity for that reception, and the preacher knowing beforehand that capacity in every man, of which many themselves are unconscious, has to induce a sympathetic attention for the Word. It is sometimes objected that we beg the premises when we ask for a predisposition to believe the Gospel. But we reply that moral affinity is the necessary medium of understanding between man and man and between man and God. We may observe this even in the case of animals relative to man; the dog or the horse understands his master through the medium of sympathy. The moral man is the man sympathetic of God, and if any man will do His will he shall know of the doctrines. And we may further answer that in fact no man approaches the religious

69

question without bias, and we are asking only that
the will should in some measure countervail the acquired instinct to reject the Gospel.

Nor can we reckon with any man entirely apart from
the community in which he has his place or the general
tendency of the age in which he lives. There have
been times in history marked in a special way with
popular readiness to receive the Gospel. On examination this readiness is found to be directly traceable to
some cause operative rather on the moral than the
mental conditions of the people. The French Revolution, for instance, produced in England an extraordinary
seriousness, which predisposed people to give attention
to the Christian ministry.

There is in South Devon a parish that still owes much
of its spiritual life to the influence of a simple devoted
woman of whom they tell a singular story. She had
been notorious as a wild profligate till the cholera of
1832 broke out in that parish, and then careless of her
life she flung herself alone into the work of nursing
the sick, and even helped the rector to bury the dead.
She survived many years later, and still her spiritual
character lives in the quiet self-controlled demeanour of
the people of her village.

In another village in Devon another woman has exercised an influence of the same kind. She, employed in a
flannel factory, met with an accident which paralysed and
deafened her, and she lost a little later the sight of one
eye. Living on parish relief, unable to hear a word or
sound, occupying a single room from which she cannot
wander, she has done more work for God in the lives of
the women and girls of her locality than can be measured.

It is a bad thing for any Church that preachers and

that doctrine. The baptismal formula contains in brief the whole faith. The preacher who wishes to teach the faith should himself consciously derive every lesson that he has to give from the one root and central truth, —Jesus is God. He need not preach or teach in such a way as to make it apparent that he is always repeating this truth in one form or another; his method ought to be so diversified as never to weary the hearer in whom, however, he studies to form the instinctive conscious-ness of the Divinity of Christ.

The great French composer Gounod has told us that his most florid and elaborate Mass music was composed on a single Gregorian tone which dominated and in-spired him. One might hear that musical service con-stantly without discovering its suggestion. And in the same way sermons, the most varied in form and char-acter, may carry the same truth and move the hearer to the desired conviction. And the most emphatic lesson conveyed by a sermon is often that doctrine which is assumed by the preacher incidentally, as it were, in the course of an approach to some other con-clusion. The hearer is not roused to resistance, and accepts as of course the incidental reference. If, for instance, the preacher is speaking of the preciousness of child-life, or of the state of the departed awaiting judgment, the arguments he would employ must come from the words of Christ in connexion with these sub-jects, and these words are cited as conclusive since He is God. Such a position should be made clear in pass-ing, without a suggestion of any kind that it is dubitable or hypothetic. John Wesley said that a sermon, in which the name of Christ was not to be found, might none the less be full of the doctrines of the Lord, whilst another with frequent mention of His name might be entirely wanting in the spirit and truth of the Gospel.

As the Sacraments of the Church are all extensions in action of the Incarnation, so the whole Christian doctrine is a deduction in thought from the Incarnation. Whether it be devotional theology or moral or dogmatic, all issues from belief in Jesus Christ as God. And if the preacher has to deal with any one or more in number, mistaken or astray in some doctrinal matter, his wisdom is to return to the source of truth, and reaffirm that in its completeness that he may then teach its implications with more accuracy. And experimentally we shall find that not only is this method right and true in theology but also that it is the practicable way.

The Gospel is for all persons, and in Christ all flesh shall see the salvation of God. But the great majority of persons cannot conceive of the abstract or academical; for these the necessary truth must be set out in personal terms. The ancient Hebrews repeatedly fell into idolatries, Egyptian, Assyrian, and Babylonian, as they found the conception of Jehovah almost unattainable. No teaching, however full, could convey to the ordinary mind the idea of God Infinite and Personal. None can come to the Father but through Christ, as the failure of the Hebrew theology amply proved. This is reaffirmed to-day by the double failure of Unitarianism to propagate itself amongst the common people, and to create the spiritual temper amongst its own adherents. God without Christ is unimaginable, whilst God in Christ is the immediate realization of every simple soul.

The textbook of theology will convey nothing to unlearned and uninstructed persons, nor would it move any that understood it to personal love and devotion. Through the Incarnation we may touch and handle the

Word of Life, and find for ourselves the motive and force of a new character. The fellowship of the faithful in Christ is something more than a number of persons holding the same view on one important subject: it is a spiritual community in one life and one mind. The mind of the Church is to be reckoned with as a medium of the guidance which the Holy Ghost gives to the redeemed. It is the mind of the Church that gave us our creeds and our Bible, and that conclusively rejected the heresies that threatened the faith.

It is through the mind of the Church that the Holy Ghost has moved again and again to revive the spiritual forces of Christendom, and to draw out in every age the necessary applications of Divine truth. But the normal function of the mind of the Church, less noted though more constant, is the absorption into orthodox devotion of all the irregular elements of opinion and intention which are to be found in the multitudes that are being added to the Church daily. We are not able to measure the extraordinary effect of the common mind of the fellowship upon the mental soul of the beginner in Christ. But it is doubtless an inspiring discipline of the first importance, and none can tell how great is the wholesomeness of the change which brings one out of conjecture, and into the common mind of that living Body which is the particular sphere of the Holy Ghost. The temper of devotion in one uninstructed is readiness of assent to the mind of the Church; it is teachableness, and acceptance beforehand of all the spiritual treasure that the Church has found in the Divine name.

The mind of the Church in its existence and effect through the ages is chiefly known under the term of tradition, though in itself it is more than mere tradition. As tradition it has a necessary part in the shaping of the Christian consciousness; naturally it puts an authoritative interpretation upon Holy Scripture. That such an interpretation is necessary may be at once learnt from the plain historical fact that any sect of Christians that has taken the Bible apart from the Church has presently disparaged the Bible itself. It is evident without argument that the Scriptures need for their full value the support of concurrent tradition and ordered discipleship. The preacher has to keep himself sympathetically in touch with this mind of the Church, as he must be its minister and channel. The newly converted and the newly awakened will need its influence and discipline and support. And in whatever condition of spiritual growth and understanding the Christian may be, the steward of the household must be ready to bring forth treasures new and old, the timely application of timeless truth.

The terms most commonly used in the New Testament for the followers of Christ may help us to know what ministry of pastoral instruction is necessary as the life in Christ advances. In the four Gospels and the Book of the Acts the Christians are called the *disciples*, and this word is restricted to these five books only. This term suggested the immediate attachment of the faithful to the person of our Lord, the great Master; it denoted those who followed Him, taking His yoke upon them, and learning of Him the meek and lowly of heart. It emphasized the personal relationship between the Lord and His people in the new life of redeemed man. It suggested discipline or method of living in obedience to the Divine will. And the preacher must encourage the sense of discipleship amongst his people, portraying the human life of Christ as the pattern for all Christians, and showing that the presence of the Holy Ghost

in the heart necessarily expresses itself in the development of Christ Jesus in the character. The Church
will then be known as the school of Christ, in which
moral instruction is authoritatively given, and there it
will be taught with no uncertain sound that neither
self-interest nor altruism is the true principle of life,
but response to the purpose of our creation. The disciple is one related subordinately to his Lord, one that
is learning how to live, one that is living so as to learn
experimentally what the true life is. In the Church the
measure of our new manhood must be set out in the
presentation of Christ the second Adam, about the
Father's business, fulfilling the Father's work, finding
it His meat and drink to do the Father's will.

But the term disciple fell suddenly into disuse, and
was followed by another word which brings another
connotation into the foreground. Repeatedly in the
Book of the Acts, and very frequently in the Epistles,
the Christians are termed *brethren*. This word is not
used before the Holy Ghost was given; it may be taken
then to express instinctive recognition of kinship through
the Holy Ghost. The brethren are those in whom the
spirit is greater than the flesh, bringing near and relating
in one household those that were naturally strangers to
one another without regard or sympathy for one another.
The word marks this recognition that those who are in
Christ are also brothers and sisters indeed, and it brings
home the lesson that none must reckon his own interests
sufficient for himself. The honour of the Christian household, the spiritual good of all that are in Christ Jesus,
the advancement of the Divine kingdom upon earth,
are the chief concern of those who know themselves as
brethren. And the Christian preacher has this ministry
also, to quicken and intensify the sense of kinship

amongst Christ's people, to teach the duty of Christian service, to inculcate the temper of spiritual association with others in the Mystical Body of Christ. It is readily recognized that the use of intercessory prayer may greatly strengthen the corporate life of the fellowship in Christ, but it is equally true that sacramental grace is an enrichment of the whole body through the particular member. The preacher must move the brethren to realize their oneness in Christ, and to put away self-consciousness and self-regard even in spiritual things, coveting earnestly the best gifts for the whole Church.

In course of time the title brethren gave place to the term *saints*; this title is found in the Book of the Acts, in the Epistles of St. Paul and of St. Jude, in the Revelation, and in the Epistle to the Hebrews. It is notable that it appears first in the New Testament in connexion with the Crucifixion: St. Matthew records, "Many bodies of the saints which slept arose and came out of the graves after His Resurrection". The word saint signifies one that is set apart and devoted to holiness. The true temper of the saints is otherworldliness. Their hunger and thirst is for righteousness; their desire is to see the King in His beauty; their affection is on things above; they seek that city whose Builder and Maker is God; they look on the things that are not seen—the eternal. Theirs is the citizenship of heaven; they live in loyalty to that government.

The instruction of the disciples and the pastoral guidance of the brethren are weighty charges, but these are not to be compared in gravity with the ministering to the saints. The guidance and inspiration of the Holy Ghost gives to the soul in grace the mystical temper, with faculties of vision and understanding which are preternatural. The preacher can-

not lightly satisfy these men with bread here in the
wilderness; their due nourishment is the greatest of
responsibilities. At first thought it might seem quite
impossible that any one sermon should be of use at the
same time to the careless and to the initiated, to the
natural man and to the spiritual, to the newly converted and to the saints; but the spoken word may in
different ways and on different levels of interpretation
reach and affect various hearts. And the saints may
derive from an immature preacher lessons of the utmost
value, and learn from him what he himself does not
know. Yet the endeavour of the preacher should be to
meet the spiritual needs of the most advanced of those
who are in the fellowship, and he must assist those
who have come to know that the things which are seen
are effects of the unseen.

It is scarcely necessary to say that the preacher will
disable his own ministry in this matter if he is evidently amongst his people as a manager or conductor
of social entertainments. It need not be denied that
smoking concerts and debating societies and holiday
clubs will bring people together, and may even make
the clergy who organize them popular. But the cost
of this popularity is altogether too great if it results
that the terms of friendship between the pastor and
the flock are wholly social and worldly. Just as great
frequency of Communion may indicate less reverence
and less devotion than very rare reception, so an easy
familiarity with the clergy as good-natured persons,
who are willing to associate with working-men on
equal terms, may mark a loss rather than a gain in
spiritual disposition or receptivity. The parson, the
recognized representative of religion, stands for something in the mind of the least instructed and most

distant of the people; he symbolizes another authority and another life. Rudimentary and incoherent as this may be, it is so far as it goes all for good. It is possible to destroy this mental attitude towards one by conduct which proves that the parson is not distant and socially superior; but the removal of the slight acknowledgment of the supernatural which exists may possibly be followed by complete indifference to all the claims of religion. The Church must always reckon with the saints and strive to fill the hungry with good things, for the saints are the conspicuous representation of Christ on earth, and the arguments of the Holy Ghost, the epistle of the Lord, read and known of all men.

And one other term applied in the New Testament merits notice; more rarely used, and yet widely, in the Book of the Acts and in the Epistles is the word *faithful* in this sense of souls in grace. The faithful are the steadfast, the loyal, the true. And the Christian preacher must encourage and promote this disposition of constancy and fidelity. There are in this connexion two results at which one should aim. The first of these is the formation of an immediate instinct of trust in God, an unquestioning readiness to accept His providence as the guidance of wisdom and love, a willingness to be abased or to be exalted, to be full or to be hungry, to abound or to suffer need. The second is the creation in the soul of that discernment which puts a spiritual interpretation on every incident in life, giving a sacramental value to the commonplace and making stones into bread.

In theory we hold that the material world is the vestment and instrument of the spiritual, but in practice we treat the things of this life as the true treasure. Our Lord has bidden us to seek first the kingdom of

God and His righteousness and to find so the relative value of all other things. It has been rightly said that Christ has given us the Divine estimate of things, their relative and proportionate values. But it is not enough to know simply of how little comparative worth are the things that we touch and taste and handle; we have to learn a more important lesson. The man of the world is making an abuse or misuse of the things of this life; that which should have ministered to his peace becomes for him an occasion of stumbling. The Buddhist and the Manichean advise the non-use of the things of this life; they counsel death in detail as the way of victory over self. The true disciple must learn the right use of the physical in the service of the spiritual. Once more we turn back to the life of God Incarnate to find the wholesome and healthful co-ordination of the natural and the spiritual. The ready obedience of the sea to Jesus Christ, wind and storm fulfilling His word,—the quickened processes of nature which gave water as wine without the means of a vine stock and the interval of six months,—the service of a fish, lowliest of sensate things, providing a tribute for the Temple, highest application of material wealth,—illustrate a harmony of all created things in the purpose of God.

Christ evidently used the physical as a means to an end always of a spiritual character. He made use of the order of nature in parable and sacrament, showing men that the whole world is an exposition of Divine wisdom and love, and may be in its most intractable elements a medium of the highest spiritual life. In His miracle of Siloam He made clay the vessel of light for one born blind. And as the soul advances in the school of Christ spiritual discernment passes into spiritual enrichment, the parable in natural things yield-

6

ing more and more to their sacramental value. The highest use of matter is the sacramental, and this is its typical use. Just as in the spiritual life the set and appointed hours of prayer increase in number till all occasions and formalities are lost and abandoned in the mystical life, so with the advance of spiritual discernment the sacramental is recognized as the true function of all use and relationships in the sphere of the physical. God presses in upon the soul through all the avenues of sense, and grace may be received through any circumstance of human experience. Matter is only form and sign and means; the spiritual is the substantial, the enduring, the real. And sometimes men that have caught a glimpse of this delight to trace the natural law in the spiritual world, and so they miss the truth that the spiritual law is eminent and paramount, and operative in the natural world. The man of spiritual discernment regards the natural and physical in this light; he will not divide between his religion and his ordinary experience. He knows himself to be in God's school on earth, learning at first hand the truth and goodness of God, and coming to know the things that belong to his peace. The truth that we come to know is precious, but not more precious than the personal attainments that we have made as we have acquired the truth. And we shall have learned the greatest of lessons when we have come to know that the common circumstances of life are a transparency of the spiritual and the Divine.

Probably the slightest ground upon which one may seem to be Christian is that of habit. Attendance at church may have no religious or spiritual value; it may conceivably be merely social or domestic in motive and purpose. In recent years church attendance as a social custom has very greatly decreased; but it is possible that this marks an advance in the spirit of religion amongst our people. The temper of unreality and of unconscious hypocrisy is bred amongst people generally when the services of the Church are for many a meaningless routine. Probably we should reckon as the gravest disasters which the Church has suffered in history the donation of Constantine and the conversion of nations as nations. The patronage of the unconverted world, and the undue distension of our congregations by the addition of masses of raw heathen, cannot add to the strength or purity of the Church of Christ. We must dread the stagnant adherent who is only a stranger in Jerusalem, and knows not what great things come to pass there in these days. Attendance at church for such persons may only add to their distance from God as they become more callous by familiarity with sacred things. And if Hezekiah was condemned by God and reproved by the prophet because he showed the Babylonian messengers all his precious things, the silver and the gold, and the spice, and the precious ointment, we perhaps shall not be held blameless when we expose too lightly the Divine mysteries to the casual and worldly and sceptical.

Probably few persons would in these days desire that any should attend the services of the Church or religious meetings on the ground of social habit ; but there is another danger which threatens. Pleasure is now offered as the inducement for attendance, and the appeal is made frankly to the sensuous and the emotional. The gratification of the natural appetites and senses has been from the beginning the strongest lure to sin, and the Christian discipleship begins with self-renunciation and self-mortification as its primary elements. Persons brought together to enjoy music

6 *

or to be thrilled by the sensational or the sentimental are not disposed to receive the Gospel of truth and self-denial ; if the sermon takes the note of its surroundings the preacher will flatter his hearers, and give them an opiate when they need drastic medicine and cautery. It is important that we do not lower the value of the Gospel in these days. The manner of an obsequious preacher, the unfortunate hireling of those people with the itching ears who will not endure sound doctrine, misrepresents God and understates the value of truth. And the rivalry in England amongst the exponents of religion gravely imperils the right appraisement of the truth of the Gospel ; the natural man who finds himself competed for by two or three adjacent ministers comes to regard religion as a form of flattery which he can command.

It is necessary from the beginning to claim the services of men under the term of duty. Life itself is a gift, and of all creatures the human child is most dependent upon parents and teachers. We are in debt and under obligation to others for all that we enjoy. As soon as a man begins to recognize his indebtedness to God he is already on the way to perfection in Christ. The man for whom one has least hope is that man who assumes that he came into existence by accident, and may live to gratify his bodily passions. It is not by chance that the centurion at Capernaum showed greater faith than any in Israel, or that another centurion at Cæsarea, Cornelius by name, gave to the Christian Church the first Gentile household. Military discipline was in these men the foundation of personal character, and their sense of duty was the dominant note in their lives. They are both conscious of their unworthiness, attentive to the welfare of others, and apprehensive of the goodness and power of God; these are the finest principles of human nature, and open the way for the coming of the Holy Spirit.   From the most elementary acknowledgment of God's existence to the highest act of worship all that God asks of us is duty.   When we have done all those things which are commanded us we can only say, we are unprofitable servants, and we have done that which was our duty to do.

The preacher has not only to give instruction; he has also to exhort his people.   Exhortation is encouragement to action, and duty is that form of service that man ought to give to God.   The preacher has not to define or prescribe the particular service in detail which this or that man must render; he should rather cultivate the spirit of duty, and leave to men severally the responsibility of scheming and planning their lives in the presence of God.   The Christian life is not a tale of tasks or total of conduct, and no routine of prescribed actions is sufficient.   The soul must be brought into healthful relations with God; as David, I have set the Lord alway before me, or as Isaiah, I saw also the Lord sitting upon a throne high and lifted up, so the soul must have the immediate recognition of the sovereignty of God, and must reflect that into the details of daily life. The preacher may be sure that the well-instructed and rightly exhorted disciple will not let himself off easily, but that the best result will follow when the soul has been taught to ascertain at first hand the will of God and to seek directly for grace to do that will.   The man in Christ is a member of the Mystical Body and not a parasite or vampire of a human teacher.

Duty is response to authority, and the whole Christian religion stands on authority.   In St. Matthew's Gospel we find this most clearly; throughout the

Gospel this Evangelist traces the fulfilment of type and prophecy in the person of Christ the King. He gives us as the climax of the Gospel the meeting of the risen Lord with His disciples on the appointed mountain in Galilee. Their commission for the conversion of the world was given by the Lord on the ground of His authority: "All power is given unto Me in heaven and in earth: Go ye therefore into all the world, preach and baptize". And the preacher is faithful to his commission when he teaches all that Christ commanded, and proclaims the kingdom of God, that he may bring all men into the obedience of Christ.

CHAPTER VI.

SOCIAL CONDITIONS.

THE Christian prophet has to preach the Word to men
of all sorts and conditions. He needs to know men
sympathetically; that is to say he must make patient
study of the circumstances which may help or hinder
the hearing and receiving of the Gospel. It is well
known that different preachers are able to affect different
classes of hearers; we speak for instance of one who is
a specialist with fishermen, another with soldiers, and
another with students. It is comparatively rare that
the specialist finds his opportunity, and it is necessary
that we all apply ourselves to the task of addressing
effectively people committed to our charge of whatever
class they may be. There are none entirely inaccessible;
and we may begin with the assurance that any channel
of affection or duty, of honesty or self-sacrifice, may
become an avenue through which truth and grace shall
gain the heart.

The study of the social and personal conditions of life is a necessary part of the preacher's preparation for his work. It is as important as the knowledge of words, for such a direct understanding enables the preacher to give his message to the soul. Some teachers have advised the reading of modern fiction for this purpose; but with very few exceptions our novelists misunderstand and mis-state life. Far more interesting and far more edifying than fiction is life itself, and the preacher ought to get as close to that as possible. It will be necessary for this end that he should lay aside all affectation and seek to know men as they are without pose or professionalism. He should avoid those who use religious phrases, and gain as much suppleness of mind as possible by talking with persons of all classes and modes of thought. There have been monographs written on the Trial and Death of Christ from both the legalist and medical point of view. This may give us some suggestion of the task which falls to the Christian prophet; he must be ready to put his Gospel into the terms of any social class, and to bring it home effectively to any person through the channels of experience and common association.

In the development of personal character the most potent cause is employment, and there is no legitimate occupation that does not form some good quality in the heart. The classes of employment amongst us are four in number, broadly defined. The first of these is agriculture,—the second professional and personal services,—the third manufacturing, mechanical and mining,—the fourth trade and distribution. That these employments attract to themselves severally persons of distinct predispositions is clear from the common observation that in a population of mixed nationalities like that of the

United States this classification falls out on racial lines.
It is there found that the Irish go almost invariably to
personal service, the Germans become bakers, butchers,
cigar-makers, wood-workers, tailors, the Jews are almost
all commercial.   Agriculture is wider and more general
in attraction, and more profound and distinct than any
other employment in its effect on character.   Its natural
tendency is to develop trust and patience ; tilling the
ground brings man into co-operation with God in those
processes which affirm God's constancy and beneficence.
And in such interaction and co-operation with God
the simple man attains stability of character and self-
restraint.   It is true of course that rural life is not all
Arcadian, but we are considering now what influences are
for good in agricultural employment ; we may recognize
in their due place the evil effects of fairs, and petty village
life, and loose conditions of hiring and housing of servants
in farm-houses.   At this point we only note the moral
advantage that still attaches to such work as God assigned to man before the fall.

Agriculture and fishing stand in marked contrast to
textile and chemical industries and type-setting and
railway employment ; all of these tend to produce
nervous disease and to shorten life.   And the man of
disordered nerves has a biassed view of God and the
world, by which he is so much the less able to receive
and assimilate the Gospel.   Amongst professional men
in England there will be commonly found a ready recognition of the sanctity of duty and some professional
honour.   And as the essence of religion lies in the recognition of the relationship between God and man,
persons who are employed in agriculture or in professional services have within themselves a natural clue to
religious truth.   By way of understanding this better

one may take the contrasting character of a person who
lives on aleatory gains, as for instance the hotel waiter
or the bookmaker.   These, it has been noticed, derive
from the uncertainty of their income great improvidence
and instability of temper; conception of the judgment
and eternal consequence seems for them impossible.
And any employment that is anti-social in character,
giving to life the spirit of rivalry and conflict rather
than of mutual service, tends to harden and isolate the
soul, and in that degree to hinder the reception of the
Gospel.

It is further notable that there is great distinction in
this matter between industrial occupations and commercial.   The mechanic or artisan has more self-possession
and true self-respect than the trader or shopkeeper,
since he is able to produce and construct something
of use or value to the community, whilst the dealer
buys and sells.   And the mind of one who buys and sells
develops alertness and self-interest and the instinct of
solitariness.   Employments which are inconstant and
over-speculative create a sceptical character, for inevitably the gambler assumes chance to be the lord of his universe.   Employments that give physical extension and
exercise promote a temper of kindness and even-minded-
ness, whilst those vocations which keep a man cramped
and confined commonly induce discontent and severity
of judgment.   It is proverbial that the blacksmith or
wheelwright in an ordinary English village is commonly good-natured and kindly, whilst the tailor or
shoemaker is critical and contentious.   Law has arbitrarily decreed that butchers shall not serve on juries in
capital cases, for it is presumed that they will be predisposed to condemn prisoners to death; but in fact they
are very generally men of humane temperament, and it is

said from experience that the tailor or shoemaker is far more severe towards the accused.

Necessarily a great religious change has passed over this country in the course of those centuries which have witnessed the growing up of large classes of salaried officials and the immense increase of irregular workers. In the feudal order every man had his inevitable place, and instinctively recognized an ascending scale in which God was supreme Sovereign. We are totally removed from that to-day, and in many minds there is no social plan or moral structure, and no room or necessity for God.

It does not need to be said that there are some conditions of work which destroy the moral capacity necessary for the reception of truth. Fraudulent enterprises and dishonest business practices sterilize the soul, and industries which bring together in immediate co-operation men and girls appear to be destructive of moral balance. Probably some trades that have an ill name are not much more pernicious for those employed in them than some others which are considered safe and respectable ; but they attract and enlist the reckless, and it is to be remarked that the popular odium attaching to any business is itself detrimental to the spiritual life of those engaged in that business as it disposes men to accept a low moral standard for themselves.

And apart from the directly moral effect of any employment we may note mental results which help or hinder. In large factories and industrial companies work-people cannot enter into their duties with as real an interest as formerly, since organization and sub-division of labour have made the workman a mere particle of a great monster, and the operative or hand is no longer an artist producing evident and complete masterpieces, but a mechanic turning out monotonously nuts, or bolts, or screw-heads. Such a person is not developed mentally but stupefied by his employment. The throb of the great engine becomes the pulse of his character. In one of our great northern cities where woollen and cotton mills stand side by side it has been remarked that the operatives engaged in these several factories are distinguishable in the street as they move. If two mills, one woollen and the other cotton, are loosed, as the phrase is, at the same moment the cotton workers overtake the woollen whose slower tread is due to the heavier movement of the weaving frames in their mill. The employment of fixed routine effaces individuality, and produces a monotonous uniformity of dull character.

As soon as any nation or class of people has passed out of that purely docile and tractable stage which marks the beginning of settled social order it is necessary to push them forward to reasoned conclusions. It is futile to bewail their lack of teachableness; they are still teachable, but no longer through the former methods and with the former sanctions. The truly difficult state is that in which people can ask questions but cannot understand answers. As soon as any person has learned to read it becomes desirable that he should learn to think, and consequently occupations that stimulate intelligence and provoke inquiry are advantageous to the soul's welfare.

The conditions of employment most happy for the formation of religious convictions are those which give regularity of work, congenial in character and with fair remuneration, developing mental qualities of reflection and forethought, with a consciousness of service to mankind, and entailing co-operation with others higher and lower in the social scale. The modern tendency of industrial and commercial life to make the rich richer and the poor poorer is disastrous alike to religion and morality. And usually sudden or abrupt changes of fortune or circumstance do not promote the spiritual disposition or make the soul more amenable to religious influences. There are some exceptions to this general rule, and it is to be observed then that these are almost invariably in cases of misfortune or suffering.

It sometimes happens that chemical elements cannot combine till some new element is added, and in experience we shall find that the additional element which most often brings a right harmony into human character is suffering. Easy conditions of life, and luxurious circumstances, are morally enervating and put a man into a wrong attitude towards his fellow-men, and consequently towards God. The Christian ideal of a social order is that in which the main body of the people are in competence without affluence, in comfort without luxury, with none so poor as to be for sale, and none so rich as to be able to buy their fellow-men.

Employment is the strongest factor in the formation of character, but social influences run it very close. These are first felt in the child-life, and here in two forms, heredity and environment. Neither of these may be disregarded when we are making an estimate of the things that count, but the two are very often over-rated. It is part of the common jargon to affirm that human character is wholly the product of heredity and environment, but this is a mask of moral cowardice easily torn off by reason or experience. Doubtless heredity contributes much to the elemental qualities of the mental soul, and the home training usually seconds and redoubles the same qualities that are derived from the parents; but personal character is not a mere mixture or compilation. An architect of recent times was known to achieve always his greatest successes when he had to build on a difficult site or in a cramped area, and the greatest characters have often owed little to favourable circumstances. There is a phenomenon in heredity called atavism; it is the recurrence of a former trait or type after a succession of generations in which that type has been unknown. Atavism is usually noticed only in the physical, but it exists no doubt also in the mental and moral. And its existence suggests that heredity does not impose a fixed group of qualities, but that it rather offers a wide range of possibilities to the heir of all the generations. Personal character in its development takes up and fructifies with selection and variability some of these possibilities.

Any direct influence upon an impressionable person may determine selection and so materially affect the formation of character. The preacher may assist by his ministry the causes which result in complete personality; he may encourage the development of ideal. He becomes part of the environment and may be a principal part. But it is necessary to notice that the social influences vary in force in different localities; there are some districts in which the domestic affections are so intense as to make a fusion of character in the community, and in transmission from generation to generation. There are parts of England in which parental love is the dominant note in the character of the village people, and there are other parts in which there is practically no direct link between the father and the children. But in general, in one degree or another, all persons are affected by society and by the general mind which is evolved by the common

experiences and feelings of all.   In the shaping of
life's course every one comes under the influence of the
common convictions and common sentiments which
run on with modifications and fresh accessions from
age to age.

There is a period in life which is nominally given to
schooling; it is commonly over-rated in the matter of
education.   Herbert Spencer was probably right in believing that the system of compulsory education is ex-
erting just the very opposite influence from that which
was intended.   It is stamping out mind by a compulsory production of equality.   It decreases the reasoning
powers by an increase in the faculty of memory or receptivity; the memory is stuffed with facts such as can
be produced successfully at a competitive examination,
and the mind is rendered incapable of reasoning and
generalization.

And our modern journalism reflects and re-acts upon
this shallow mental restlessness, and is taken to be
sufficient literature by many who can read but who
cannot think.   It is singular that any persons can suppose that ability to read or write is in itself a moral or
mental gain; such acquirements bring possibilities of
good or evil, and the use made of these acquirements
determines their profit or loss to the mind and soul.   We
need not doubt that ultimately the wider extension of
the rudiments of knowledge will tend to good, but at
present we are in a confused state of more loss than
gain.   A great river completely frozen or wholly free is
a highway of commerce, and ships or sleighs may pass
upon it, but in a time of thaw or of half-frost traffic is
impossible.   So personal devotion and religion may
exist in the entirely ignorant or in the learned, but
in the ignorant that thinks he is learned there is

apparently little conception of God or self. And now conceit of knowledge exists where knowledge does not, and the assumption of learning is clouding many a mind against the light, and a hardly compelled knowledge of a few elementary subjects has brought in moral deterioration, conceit and scepticism, pretentiousness and cynicism. Education ought to befit the learner for his life's duty, and it needs to be therefore a particular adjustment of the person to the community. In the measure in which one is rendering service to others, one is open to the Divine influences and gifts.

But further, there is in almost every one a bias or prejudice which must be reckoned with. You will find, for instance, a district in the United States in which universalism is the general religious mind. If you make inquiry there you may learn that this position has been reached only by revolt against Calvinism which formerly held the ground. And similarly Unitarianism in some northern cities of England is a reaction against Presbyterianism, and has no constructive or positive theology of its own. Often the children of a harsh religious father prove this rule in their own persons, and we can have nothing but sympathy for a child that grows up alienated from a God caricatured.

But not only have we to recognize the moral difficulties caused by revolt and reaction in the soul; we have to note a further moral indisposition. The man self-satisfied and complacent is almost beyond hope, and this state is due to a disproportion of knowledge and ideals. Repentance is quickened in the soul by bringing into contrast the goodness of God and the sinfulness of self; and where self is over-rated and God and duty ignored self-satisfaction reigns. Now the conditions of our times flatter the natural man; he is too readily unconscious of anything lacking in his mental or moral equipment.   He is on easy terms with himself and simpers through life.   These have no depth of soil and for a while they may believe, but in time of temptation they fall away.   The most frequent moral cause of neglect of the Gospel is probably this,—the simple nescience of the soul's need and God's goodness.   Concerning such a man one may ask, Did this man sin or his parents that he was born blind?   Probably his parents were greatly in fault, and he is a partaker of their sins.

It is commonly recognized that the reckless and abandoned are morally indisposed for the Gospel.   But the student of social and personal conditions must be patient to distinguish amongst moral defects that he may learn the meaning of the Lord's declaration, " The publicans and harlots go into the kingdom of God before " the chief priests and elders of the people.   There are some great depravities which come of qualities which are not culpable.   St. Augustine refers to the fact that drunkenness ruins the best rather than the worst of men, as birds steal good fruit rather than bad.   Sociability and the spirit of comradeship may bring a man to ruin where a meaner or more selfish man would have walked safely.   And the flagrant faults of publicans and harlots are less perilous for the soul than the studied obliquities and calculated scepticisms of chief priests and scribes.   The ecclesiastical temper with its associations seriously endangers the spiritual life.   From the patron who is courted by clergy to the sexton whose continued employment depends upon a certain exterior respectability the traffic of the temple desecrates alike the soul and the Church.   And when we question what moral defect most hinders the spiritual life we shall

7

come to dread chiefly that which hardens the heart and leaves the sinner unconscious of his peril.

Influences which set the individual life in healthful relations to the community may be reckoned of advantage to spiritual character. If we make comparison of men living in conditions of isolation, with others living in ordinary social life, we shall notice that there are certain qualities which for their existence depend upon social relationships. Social conditions largely determine for the individual what elements of his personality shall be effective, what suggestions shall influence his thoughts, his feelings, and his decisions. In the man isolated many elements must remain latent. It cannot be said that every kind of social life is conducive to higher morality ; it is well known that in densely populated towns, and in districts which are making the transition from agriculture to industry, the criminal temper is frequently found. But a well-ordered social life is the best sphere within which the spiritual may be developed. Society evokes the best and restrains the worst in the individual, and this is the mainspring of all high morality. The isolated man becomes selfish and unrestrained ; he is naturally inconsiderate and improvident. He lacks the sense of responsibility and is apt to live as though he were the centre of his universe, and should have no successor.

Marriage and parentage put the man at once into the life of the community and also into line with ancestry and posterity ; the common life and the continuous stream of life gather him into association with immeasurably wide interests. He instinctively accommodates himself to the wishes and habits of others, and finds himself happier in the service he renders to others than in the gratification of his own animal desires.

He has to reckon with the welfare even of the unborn, and to know that his own unrestraint or self-indulgence may confront him for life in the disease or deformity of a child blameless. Half the heathen virtues and all the Christian are suggested by fatherhood, which is itself a likeness to God. And the social life, though it has the family for its unit, is larger than the family; it groups in families of families, and so makes the nation. In the larger ranges of the social state we find the completer stratification of superiors, equals, and inferiors, and a right adjustment to all these classes is a great moral discipline and education. It has been often observed that the most important result of public school and university life is found, not in the measure of scholarship attained, but in the development of character in terms of harmonious comradeship and due recognition of authority.

Religious influences may run along the lines of duty and authority very naturally; but it is notable that grace often flows from lower to higher levels of society. Whilst the ordinary social influence of a master upon his servant seems to be strong and direct the conversion of the master by his man is the more common rule. Brother Laurence is the typical instance of a servant full of grace, exercising a wide ministry amongst his social superiors. And not rarely in England we find the faithful servant, the gardener or groom, who half-unconsciously is guide and priest to many in his master's household.

But it is a mistake to suppose that the normal order is from child to parent rather than from parent to child; and the assumption that parents are to be approached and attracted to religion through their children has had and is having disastrous results. First, the attempt to

7 *

reach parents through the children is usually sentimental in character, and the appeal is made to the
children on the ground of interest or amusement. The
value and importance of religion are necessarily under-
stated in such a case, and religion is then a childish
thing to be outgrown and abandoned at manhood or
womanhood. Experience shows that persons who have
been brought to church by their children are rarely
convinced disciples, and that children who have brought
their parents to church are in danger of being patroniz-
ing in their attitude towards both Church and parents.
The proposal that we should direct our ministry chiefly
to the children is gravely mistaken : we ought to claim
the children through the parents and urge the parents
to do their duty by their children. Far too much has
been said of the importance of the early years of childhood ; it is possible to give numberless instances of
persons who have been brought up in the midst of definite influences which have passed entirely out of their
lives later. The suggestion that we should practically
abandon the older people, and direct ourselves almost
wholly to the attracting and entertainment of the
younger is a counsel of despair, justified neither by the
religious state of our people, nor by such results as the
plan produces. It is important that we teach the
sanctity of fatherhood and motherhood, and that in this
connexion we encourage families to come together to
church, and sit together in church.

It is important that we affirm definitely the priesthood
of the head of the house. Some movements of our times,
such as for instance the legislative grant of free education to the working classes, have weakened the sense of
parental responsibility ; and consequently little is left of
the sense of the duty of children to parents or of parents

to children.   It is not a mere accident that the word piety
which first meant filial duty has come now to bear the
sense of personal religion.

There are two principles in religion which appear at
first sight to be incompatible with one another; due deference to the authority of the Church and full recognition of the responsibility of the individual for his beliefs.
In England the second of these principles has run riot
and has been perverted into licence to think as one likes.
This in fact has brought us into a common state of disregard for the opinions of parents and teachers, and all
authority of that kind is instinctively rejected and re-
sented.   It is impossible that this should not entail
serious moral loss: If the line of approach to the soul
which is afforded by family affection is blocked, religion
has suffered a grave check and is at a disadvantage.

We ought in our ministry to be able to come at the
ordinary non-religious Englishman as the Apostles approached men of the heathen world who were under
Roman discipline or Greek influences; they confidently
relied upon certain lines of authority and certain moral
prepossessions in those to whom they addressed themselves.   But so far from that being our case we have
now to face in England such disadvantages as confront
our missionaries in South Africa; there our military
operations have broken down the iron systems of morality amongst native races which were at least effective,
and our subsequent attempts to educate the children
of the tribes have been frustrated by the moral stupor
for which we are responsible.   The displacement and
confusion with one another of the various tribes, and
their association with debased whites, have made the
work of the missionary difficult.   Similarly in this
country we have to deal with masses of raw heathen,

undisciplined hordes to whom Good Friday and Christmas Day are both alike occasions for riot and football, and for whom life has little meaning but sensual enjoyment. It is only fair to say that the case of our richer classes is rather worse, for with them there is the added difficulty of public school religion. Apparently a man may go through a public school and university course now and emerge worse than a heathen, for a heathen has not the insolence for God which an Englishman may readily acquire in his school days. The poor debased labourer is not so great a difficulty for us as the city man, the business man, whose life is full of artificial pleasures, unhealthy excitements and ignored responsibilities; when such men are our Church officers and representatives at Diocesan Conferences and in the Houses of Laymen the Church is hampered and well-nigh paralysed.

Inquiry amongst those who are at religious work will show that one great impediment in the way of Christianity to-day is the worldly temper amongst our people. The depopulation of our rural districts is a symptom of the same moral disorder.   The love of excitement moves young people to leave the villages and crowd into the towns.   And town life is for most classes unreal and unwholesome.   Quick and easy movement by electric cars, and late and ever later hours of pleasure, destroying evening prayers and preventing early rising for Holy Communion, reduce young people to animalism.   The constant excuse that there is no time for religion through the strain of business will not hold : for during these past fifty years the hours of business have been much reduced, and the conditions of employment greatly improved.   It is less than fifty years ago that some public-houses in our great cities were never closed by day or by night.   But the new tyranny which exhausts our people is that of organized entertainment, and this is far more destructive of personal religion than any servitude however severe.

Reference has been made to what might be called local climate in matters of religious feeling. This also has to be reckoned with practically. During the past fifty years in this country a wide movement has unsettled Dissent and brought great numbers of people into the Church. Though this movement has been more marked in some parts of the country than in others it is probable that it is nowhere altogether unknown or unfelt. It has been caused by increased travel and interest in history. Sir Walter Scott, Matthew Arnold, Ruskin and Carlyle have undermined the foundations upon which Dissent stood. It never had any hold upon the working-class masses in our great cities, and the fundamental and political changes through which we are now passing are threatening its credit and existence; for history shows that popular Dissent for two hundred years past has maintained itself chiefly in protest against grievances, real or imaginary, suffered by that lower middle class which gave it bulk. It was consequently at its zenith of power immediately after the first Reform Bill, which extended the franchise to members of that social group; but its political strength has been weakened by every subsequent extension of the franchise. Meanwhile the expedients by which the leaders of Dissent have tried to keep their followers together, in attacks upon religious education and the income and prestige of the Church, have detached from Dissent very many of its best people. Especially in many country districts the sincere godly members have quietly left Dissent and offered themselves for Confirmation; they find

the political temper and tyranny offensive to their sense
of religion.

Further, the two periods in the course of the nineteenth
century which were conspicuously marked by considerable developments of Dissent in our rural districts were
the first decade of that century and just fifty years later.
These were not periods of special spiritual awakening,
but of enlarged social intercourse between town and
country, occasioned by two European wars, the Penin-
sular and the Crimean. The immediate result of this
stir and movement was a disturbance of the settled
social order of the villages. And the little village causes
gained much strength and many adherents from the
new influences of the town upon the peasantry. But
facilities of travel and cheap journalism have finally destroyed the separateness of villages and now we live all
in one general national life. There may conceivably
be a future for Dissent in this country on some other
grounds, but the political and social causes that have
helped it during the past two centuries are exhausted,
and we have now to deal with a steady march of converts that approach us from that direction, well-inten-
tioned and sincere though usually uninstructed in
Christian doctrine. It must be always noted that
they come to us by repulsion from political agitation
rather than from attraction to spiritual truth, and they
have therefore to find amongst us the spiritual character
which will give them settlement and satisfaction.

And finally note must be taken of the effect upon character which is due to conditions of housing and lodging.
We may take it as axiomatic that what is bad for the
health is bad for the soul and hindering to religion.
The overcrowding of the districts in our cities which are
occupied by the working classes produces an increased

rate of mortality; and very generally those conditions which militate against good health are equally harmful to modesty and morality. It is evidently difficult to bring up a family of five or six children in a cottage with only two bedrooms, without risking the loss of proper self-respect. And in some rural districts, with less excuse, the conditions of housing are often as bad as those which prevail in our crowded cities, and children grow up with no possible privacy, and nursing mothers are treated with no more delicacy than the animals on the farm.

We must gladly acknowledge the great goodness of many landowners who have done much and are doing much to afford to their tenants healthy and comfortable dwellings of sufficient accommodation, and we must also give due credit to the enlightened policy of some of our municipalities, notably that of Liverpool, which provide model dwellings in place of the miserable hovels condemned as insanitary : but most of all must we give due meed of praise to the innumerable gentle working-class mothers who in town and country scheme and contrive somehow to eke out the straitness of their circumstances to cover and protect the modesty of their little ones. It is one of the splendours of our people that so many have forethought and patience to baffle the mischance of their poverty and to secure for their children the best results of easier fortune.

CHAPTER VII.

PERSONAL CONDITIONS.

THE study of sociology gives us some general results. We can predicate the effects in human character of great public movements, such for instance as revolutions or industrial struggles; and we can measure also something of the consequences of various kinds of employment and domestic influences. But capacity to receive the Christian doctrine is not a faculty appended to character: it is the principal function of the whole character. Man is not a being that has a special organ to receive truth: he is rather that special being that is made to have the truth of necessity if he would become himself. It follows that whatever contributes to the formation of character goes to make or mar man as the audience of God. And every single character is the resultant of more forces than you can compend in a category of work, residence, health, and education. We must go farther to find the key to individual cases. The personal gambit, the personal bias, must be reckoned with.   The gambit is the opening at chess which very often largely predisposes the course of the game, and we shall frequently find that all the incidents in a particular life are appropriated by, and assimilated with, a dominating idea which is apparently uncaused or accidental.   And if we are right in deriving "bias" from a word which makes it to mean originally a squint, we shall recognize its appropriateness in the view that many people take of their lives and circumstances. A coloured print of a greyhound might be put before three men consecutively with three different effects : one, a lithographer, would examine its production as a process of printing; another, as an artist, would criticize the draftsmanship and colour ; the third, a sporting man, would wager something upon its chance of winning a race.   But with differences less widely marked than these, of employment and class interest, similar distinctions are to be found everywhere.   We know that often children of the same parents who have been brought up in the same circumstances of poverty or wealth and with the same opportunities of study and self-development are notably unlike one another.   And we have to seek yet deeper for the causes which so assert themselves.

It is evident to every one that there are moments and sometimes longer periods when the attention is preternaturally alert and the whole mind is highly sensitized. At such times, which fall apparently under no rule of health or volition, an idea impregnates the mental soul and qualifies or conditions subsequent mental processes. Sometimes even a single word is capable of becoming the master-note of the life following.   Not seldom when inquiry is made of the particular cause of conversion one is assured that a text or a phrase has given the life new direction and new momentum.

We have therefore to consider so far as we are able the influences in life which are personal and particular. What direct causes may be found to produce an appetite for spiritual truth? That is the question to which we now address ourselves. Probably some would answer at once that the religious instruction in our day schools must reckon first in this matter with many. But it is easy to over-rate the spiritual worth of religious truths taught as school subjects; and it is even possible to produce blank atheism whilst giving instruction in strict comformity with the orthodox Creeds. The most precious right at present secured to the managers of Church schools is that of nominating the masters and mistresses in those schools: if these are chosen with great care and so treated as to help them to realize their ministry the syllabus and time-table are comparatively unimportant.

Otherwise an absolute knowledge of the plagues of Egypt and the Kings of Judah and Samaria and even of similar lists in the New Testament will assure nothing of the spiritual life in the child, and may conceivably in the course of a few years pass into oblivion with the inchoate smatterings of other sciences upon which some school time has been wasted. In the elementary schools of modern Greece the Jewish children are exempted from religious instruction but all alike enter for examination; and it is reported that the Jewish children invariably take the first places in examination as the result of overhearing the regular instruction given to other children. But such knowledge of the Christian doctrine does not make these Jews to become Christian; and the instruction in our schools, far less exact in matters of religion, does not count as a converting influence.

Our Church schools are to be justified as religious

schools by their conspicuous success in producing better
charactered children than those which are from other
schools. Employers who are quite impartial religiously
will nevertheless carefully inquire, when they have to
appoint an errand boy or an office boy, whether the
applicant comes from a Church school or otherwise;
the employer is anxious to obtain a boy who is courteous,
self-respectful and human.   We must not undervalue
such moral results as these which are produced in our
Church schools, and we must not overestimate the
spiritual results which we suppose they can command.

At adolescence, which is the most critical and impressionable period in life, there comes commonly the
gift of Confirmation preceded by a period of preparation
which is of momentous importance. We hear on every
side of the supreme value attaching to this opportunity
of dealing with young people individually and spiritually.
We may note in passing the unwisdom of proposals to
lower the age at which Confirmation is generally given.
Whilst the objective gift of grace is not dependent upon
the mental attainment of the recipient, the resultant
effect in the appropriation of that grace must depend
in large measure upon the disposition of the confirmed.
And it is practically verifiable that the preparation goes
deeper and involves more largely the mind and heart
when the catechumen has clearly passed out of childhood into maturer life.   And further, since adolescence
is the infancy of the complete personality and brings
very often with it an inclusive revolution of character, it
is a counsel of prudence which gives us the rule that
Confirmation should be administered to those who are
of age to learn the elements of the faith and to answer
for themselves with some recognition of the seriousness
of life.

It is only fair to say that many persons who have right to be considered in this matter regard the first years of adolescence as the period the least suited for Confirmation; and they would suggest that if you cannot present the candidate before puberty you would do well to postpone the preparation for some years. The ground they take is that this period is one of confusion and turbulence in the moral and mental character; and that any positive teaching that may be given is likely to be lost or distorted in the upheavals and resettlements involved in adolescence. It is customary amongst the Kosas in South Africa to allow boys for a certain short term of years to indulge themselves freely in every kind of excess and riot as irresponsible beings; and there are many writers who would argue that at the beginning of adolescence judgment and conscience may be singularly perverted. It is only fair in passing to take note of that argument, but we may add that in many cases the dawning of manhood or womanhood is unaccompanied by disturbances so profound as this theory suggests.

There are many experienced parish priests who unhesitatingly attribute the most clearly marked conversions in their parishes to this period of preparation for Confirmation. Imagine what the ordinary parish would become if there were no more instructions for Confirmation given, and Lent no longer kept. Would the spiritual life of the people as a religious community survive ten years in such conditions? The annual Confirmation is an indraft of spiritual health for the whole flock, renewing the fervour and zeal of the older as they receive into fellowship the younger; and this is an occasion similar to Lent in its emphasis of the personal and subjective in religion.

The preparation for Confirmation must be twofold in character, of head and of heart. The former part is completing and making definite all the religious lessons and impressions of childhood, that the catechumen may know what God is, what is His Will for man, and how to seek and receive help to do His Will. This part of the preparation throws the net which has to be drawn with great care or it will break. Whilst these subjects, the Creed, the Commandments, Prayer and Sacraments, are being treated the classes are gradually resettled in smaller groups and definite approach is made to the soul. If man were an unfallen creature faith in God might tolerably well express the right disposition of man towards his Maker; but since sin is the universal state from which man must be recovered by grace, repentance is the necessary way of approach to the Father. And repentance is the soul's response to Christ on Calvary.

When the second stage of the preparation is reached by further and further subdivision, groups of catechumens are brought down to ones and twos, till every one is under all the possible influences which make for spiritual decision. It might appear axiomatic that the catechumens should be finally under individual instruction, but no such rule can be wisely made. There are some persons so timid and reserved that they need the help of companionship even when receiving instruction; and there are others who unconsciously support and express the faith of their companions with their own. St. Peter illustrates this in his relations with the other apostles.

And in the preparation for Confirmation there must be established if possible an openness of conference between the soul and God. There will probably come no such opportunity later for the formation of personal and spiritual confidence. When some staggering sorrow falls upon one of our people, likely to cause insanity or suicide, the only way of salvation may be through that direct relationship which has been established in the preparation for Confirmation. That is the one occasion on which every soul separately comes into some personal touch with the pastors of the flock. The definite study of the subjects of our Catechism, the intense personal ministry under which every catechumen passes, the solemnity and gift of the Holy Ghost by the laying on of hands, make in very many cases the greatest crisis in the spiritual consciousness. Our people happily are not prone to overstate their religious experiences, and do not readily measure them for themselves. But there are countless faithful souls to whom Confirmation has meant conversion in all its completeness and with none of the attendant circumstances of self-regard which mar that spiritual movement in times of religious excitement.

And here incidentally we note the advantage that the pastor in his office of preacher may gain from this same occasion. In a former lecture we remarked that the knowledge of souls is a necessary part of the equipment of the Christian prophet. He will gain greatly in this knowledge from his experience in Confirmation classes. The psychologist in his study of the mental and moral contents of human nature finds the best opportunity in abnormal conditions, as these give increased prominence to various factors and processes. And for the student of the spiritual man the early years of adolescence afford the most valuable opportunity. The irregularity and disproportion of newly acquired faculties of thought and feeling enable the teacher to get the measure and find the value of different elements which constitute human nature. The preacher will

gain much in his pulpit ministry in sympathy, persua-
siveness, directness and the art of teaching from his
experience with catechumens.

Pastoral visitation holds the people in a less definite and looser method of instruction. We are assured by many persons and also by adages that church
attendance is promoted by pastoral visitation ; and
there are as many authorities of at least as great
weight on the other side. It is sometimes argued that
many people of the working classes regard the visits
of the clergy and district visitors as a sufficient discharge of their own duty of attending church, and this
statement is not without some show of truth. But
without affirming at once that parish visiting helps or
hinders common worship, we may weigh two considerations. The first is the social ; in some localities and
with some classes of persons undoubtedly such visitation is liked and is rightly understood, whilst in other
places and with other persons there is suspicion, and
resentment or contempt caused by this same ministry.
And the second is the pastoral : the nature of the visit
itself as an occasion for direct instruction and kindly
exhortation or as a means of friendly intercourse must
determine its value. Generally speaking, social intercourse hampers and embarrasses the spiritual ministry
unless the relationship is complete enough to include
the social within the spiritual. St. Paul's resolution
was "not to know anything among you, save Jesus
Christ and Him Crucified". As preachers and teachers
there is nothing in human nature that is foreign to us,
but we must be vigilant and jealous to subordinate all
things to the true end. When the pastor can go
directly into a house with the invocation of peace and
talk in frank simplicity with anyone that he finds there

8

of spiritual things this ministry is most valuable. It
constitutes in detail the parish class, and it gives opportunities for the particular application of the Word.
And it detracts nothing from the sacredness of divine
service and the importance of taking part in the common
worship.

The visiting of the sick falls within this division of
our ministry; and needs more than passing notice.
It is sometimes thought that sickness in a household
makes an unusually favourable opportunity for the
introduction of religion to the family or at least to
the sick person. There are, however, few matters of
pastoral interest upon which there is a more absolute
consensus of opinion amongst the experienced and ob-
servant than this; resolutions made on a sick-bed are
never kept, and religion rarely if ever enters by this
way. And where promises of amendment have been
made and broken it sometimes happens that the cause
of religion suffers from the resentment of a man who
feels that advantage was taken of his weakness to
pledge him to reform. For many reasons sickness is
not the best time for the process of conversion, and
the visitation of sick persons must not be contemplated
as a means of adding to the Church those that should
be saved. But this is not to say that no good can be
done in visiting the sick. Much may be done by way
of helping those who are in grace and in discipleship.
The time of sickness may be kept by a man in grace
as a retreat, limited and conditioned of necessity by
circumstances which restrict his freedom of mind or
hinder the advised occupation of his time. Under
careful guidance days or even weeks may be spent
profitably, and habits of devotional study and meditation established.

There are other occasions less constant and regular than these to which we have referred, and yet it may be of surpassing importance to the individual. The ordinary parish administration is sometimes helped and reinforced by a mission or revival. It is well to use these terms if we may synonymously; the word mission connotes for us the divine origin of the movement which brings us a special offer of truth and grace, whilst the word revival connotes the necessary life-giving helps of the Holy Spirit upon which the whole result depends. The word revival has fallen into discredit because it has become associated with unrestraint and emotionalism, but we must recover it to its right use.

A mission is an enterprise of so great an importance that it should be arranged only after the greatest deliberation. It is impossible for a mission to be held with no result; if it does not bring help and renewed life to a parish it will certainly do positive harm. A mission may be followed by a chill or a reaction from which the best hope of recovery is in a change of incumbents. A mission ought not to be held frequently in any parish; it should come as a rare and singular undertaking, claiming the attention and response of all people in the parish.

The season of Lent may readily be used for courses of special preaching and even for consecutive days of doctrinal instruction. Advent too may be in some places convenient for unusual appeals to the people. The wise use of these seasons will leave the term mission free for application to a great work of some days' duration in which the whole parish is concerned. It must first be recognized that the mission is held with definite purpose; it is desired to intensify the spiritual life of the flock and to add to their number many who have been living as heathen. Nothing of ritual or parochial organization

8 *

should be added during the mission or immediately after its conclusion ; its effect must be to fulfil and to stimulate and rekindle and reinforce.   The preacher who is to conduct the mission should be carefully chosen.   In the midst of profound movements of heart and mind he has to keep the proportions, encouraging spiritual intuition and restraining self-assertion and over-confidence.   He has to stand between the living and the dead—to discern between the movements of the Holy Spirit and the simulations of Satan.   He has to recognize with immediate apprehension the first note of hysteria and to stay it resolutely.   And he must be prepared to make any necessary decision without hesitation even to the length of closing the mission abruptly.   If we believe in revival as well as mission, and approach the whole enterprise with constant and united intercessions, we shall be ready to take any course that is manifestly suggested by the Holy Spirit.   The apparent failure of a mission is nothing against it ; its abounding popularity and successes in its early days should cause hesitation.   A true missioner will not allow himself to be extravagantly praised and will doubt his fidelity to his Master when all speak well of him.

It should not need to be said that the subject-matter of a mission is the Atonement.   If the normal life of the Church were sound and healthful a mission would never be necessary.   This is a method of supplement necessitated by something lacking in the spiritual life of the flock.   And that which is lacking is the complete sense of reconciliation with God, and personal life fulfilling that relationship.   Therefore the Atonement is the one great subject of mission preaching.   But it must be understood that the right preaching of the Atonement requires far-reaching reference and

demands definite and vivid teaching concerning God
and man. So that in truth when we say that the
Atonement must be preached we really mean that the
Gospel must be proclaimed with this emphasis and this
reiterated application.

The first days of a mission are devoted usually to an
endeavour to promote a consciousness of sin amongst
the people ; and sometimes this division of the mission
course may occupy two-thirds or three-fourths of all
the days. Local circumstances must determine this
matter. The persuasions of the Love of God summed
up in the Cross are not to be offered to complacent or
self-satisfied persons; the law must precede the Gospel, and salvation must be proclaimed to those who
know their need. A hundred years ago teaching concerning the Atonement was comprised in terms very
few and incomplete. The work of Christ in the salvation of man was set out with little regard to His personality and life. And the position of the convert was
consequently that of a recipient of benefits which had
come to him at the cost of another. The more
balanced teaching which sets before us Christ as the
Revealer of the Father and the Pattern for the brethren
diminishes nothing of the adoring love which is due to
Him as the Saviour of mankind. The several offices and
ministries of Christ are not competing in exclusion of
one another ; to know Him in any relationship more
fully is to understand Him better in all relationships.
And in a mission whilst the Atonement is the perpetual
theme, the personality of our Lord, His Incarnation,
His whole Humanity, His Eternal Sonship, His present
Ministry in the heavens, all have their due place ; and
all are to be pressed home to conclusions in the lives of
the faithful. A mission is of practical character ; it aims

at producing results in the spiritual nature. The missioner must never lose sight of the purpose, nor turn aside to achieve any temporary successes.

There is good reason to believe that at the present time very much may be done for good in informal talks with men in ordinary social sets. This is probably easiest when the talk arises from a question asked or a suggestion made by one of the company casually. It is notable that the great parables in St. Luke's Gospel are elicited by some casual word addressed to our Lord. They are not in the set form of those narrated by St. Matthew or St. Mark. The most direct teaching given in the third Gospel breaks out in response to a touch : " And who is my neighbour ? " brings us the story of the Good Samaritan ; " Speak to my brother that he divide the inheritance with me," gives the parable of the Rich Fool. Certain it is that Englishmen are very shy on religious subjects, but they rather welcome than resent frankness if it is plainly unpretentious and unprofessional. And very often in a few words questioners may be helped to become thinkers, and a stray soul may be in the net if not yet drawn to the shore. In matters of religion the ordinary English professional man reads the reviews instead of listening to the sermons, and the preacher would be ill-advised if he tried to deal with review articles in the pulpit. The informal talk of half a dozen men together where one knows his position and has reached it by conviction, and where the talk is unforced and the touch light, is worth fifty sermons. The modern preacher, so far from resenting a critical allusion to his sermons or his Church, should avail himself gladly and alertly of the opportunity of learning something and teaching something.

But a mission differs in one great characteristic from

the informal occasion. In a mission the preacher uses the common feeling of a mass of people to unsettle and break up various fenced positions of the people that form the congregation. The first work to be done in a mission is this; the gradual deposits which have silted up the channels of the soul must be swept away by a profound disturbance of feeling and conviction. The missioner intentionally or instinctively avails himself of the momentum and sweep of the common mind in action to get the moral impact necessary for the individual. This noteworthy movement may be observed in any well-developed mission; persons that have lived isolatedly with no interest in their neighbour's affairs, are consciously brought into community of feeling with others of entirely different habits of character. This common feeling, and it is little more than feeling, clears the ground for new beginnings in personal life; probably if one who followed a mission so far and had reached this experience were then to be suddenly removed to another parish the result in that case would be prejudicial rather than beneficial to personal religion.

The advantage of the state reached through the opening stages of the mission depends upon and must be made good by the further and more constructive methods of the later stages. The preacher must have before him the purpose of leaving all the people that are reached by the mission in a tranquil and teachable disposition. The last note of the mission should be not primarily thanksgiving but confident intercession. And the lasting effect of the mission should be a readier acceptance of the Word, with an implicit acknowledgment of the Sovereign Authority of Jesus Christ. A calm agreement with all that are in Christ and unhesitating belief in the truth of the Gospel should be the temper produced by a mission. The scene at Gadara expresses it all in figure ; at first the man of divided will, and then the storm of prayer and protest, and last the new disciple sitting at the feet of Jesus clothed and in his right mind.

The use of memorial cards or of any other external sign of decision or conscious spiritual progress during a mission is by way of marking a point from which there must be no retrogression.   An overt act or tangible object, a cross or a card or a medal, fixes the impression and makes it no longer merely mental or verbal. A mission should give to the convert emancipation, light, and momentum.   As in the deliverance of St. Peter from prison, the new man should be awakened, set free, guided into liberty and brought into the company of the Church where many are gathered together praying.

In this connexion we take note of catechizing, a form of instruction usually but not necessarily restricted to children.   Catechism has been a method of the Church from the time of Origen and the famous catechetical school of Alexandria in the third century.   To the catechism of St. Cyril we owe some of the terse phrases in our Nicene Creed.   And these two references may help us to put a right appreciation upon the method of catechism.   By means of question and answer in set forms you ensure dogmatic instruction and exact definition.   The question provokes interest and commands attention for the answer, as a harrow breaks the clods for the reception of seed.   The answer is not only heard but repeated by the hearers and so is redoubled in its effect on the mind.   And the volume of sound when many repeat the answers simultaneously further helps the memory and deepens the confidence of those who learn.   It is in a small way the consensus

of the faithful.   It is important that in all these forms
of instruction the answer repeats as much of the question as is necessary to make a complete grammatical
statement.   The answers alone throughout the whole
chapter of catechism should be a continuous intelligible
instruction.

A mixed congregation of adult persons may be taught
by this method under certain conditions.   The church
must be one in which sound travels so well as to allow
the catechist to hear the most diffident speaker.   Already
in many parts of England parents attend children's services, and these parents are very ready to acknowledge
how much they have learned from such attendance.
And more rarely, though with even greater advantage
in some parts of England, catechizings take place after
the second lesson at Evensong on Sunday night.   A
small group of well-instructed children sit in readiness
at some distance from the pulpit, and are questioned in
the hearing of all the people.   It is necessary to make
the preparation for this beforehand with great careful-
ness that the children may know the line of teaching
that will be taken and the kind of answers that will be
expected.   And the catechist may then quicken the interest of the people sufficiently to be able by an adroit
diversion to evoke answers from the general congregation or at least to induce the people as a body to repeat
together the final summaries of the children's lesson.
Catechizing in this fashion should not occupy more than
ten minutes and is not in place of the ordinary sermon.

It will be found that persons who have lived in a
parish during a period of serious change in the doctrinal
bases of parish administration are commonly better
instructed than those who have never known a discussion on any theological matter.   And no doubt

some of our modern controversies have brought into the foreground some questions of doctrine and Christian belief. But this is an accidental and disproportionate presentation of religious truth, and even so far as it seems to give a knowledge of doctrine it is generally out-weighed by a loss of charity and receptivity. And any means or occasion that seems to promise an immediate gain in the measure of knowledge should be used or accepted only when it is clear that there will be no corresponding disadvantage in the matter of temper and the spiritual life. Apparently we cannot hope to bring the whole people of an ordinary town parish into discipleship, but we may confidently strive to secure that every one in the parish respects the Church as that supernatural society which witnesses for God, and to which any one may turn for help and guidance when penitent and sincere.

There are particular occasions that invite the intervention of the clergy and seem to promise great results to our ministry, as, for instance, a family quarrel or arrest of a son or daughter, the bankruptcy or suicide of the head of the house; and the pathetic or passionate appeal made in such circumstances is, of course, heard and heeded with sympathy. Let us not deceive ourselves; on such occasions we are consulted as kind neighbours or reliable friends whose social integrity is above suspicion, but our ministry gets no opportunity. At the most you may break down a prejudice or get an introduction for later use, but it is so rare as to be almost unknown that a religious revival in personal or family life has sprung from such a cause. If some gross vice has induced nausea as when a drunkard finds himself broken and loathsome, that state must not be mistaken for penitence; and if the pledge of total abstinence is taken by one in such a condition it ought to be for a short probationary term. By gradual extension this may be brought into a period of sober reflection, and repentance may be encouraged in that period, and eventually the spiritual life result. But preaching to drunken persons or pressing a maudlin to professions of religious experience is entirely without justification. And we may add that for similar reasons a strong restraint must be exercised when a preacher is speaking in the open air, or to persons of greatly varied opinions on religion in any common assembly. It is due to the preciousness of revealed truth that the Divine Name should be used with economy, and no lavish offers of love and pardon be made to those who have never felt contrition or compunction.

Personal misfortune and long-protracted troubles frequently have good moral results in character. This is the paradox in life which the writer of fiction commonly fails to notice. It is not true generally that people are embittered by misfortune, or that the feeling that life is not worth living is to be found amongst those who have nothing, rather than amongst those who have everything. The question whether misfortune will help or hinder the development of moral character must depend upon personality, the qualities which reject or appropriate, which discern and interpret. But it has been noticed that ill-health and physical suffering turn more often to good, whilst loss of property and failure in business tend in the other direction. A man that has an invalid wife or an imbecile child might in a group of six or eight men in familiar discussion together be found out by the human note of his part in the conversation; some qualities of character of the very highest rank spring naturally from personal misfortune bravely endured. It is not necessary to say, however, that there are certain classes of disease which cause great depression and directly produce melancholy; in such conditions the patient can only be regarded with the utmost pity.

And last in the consideration of personal conditions we note the largest and deepest distinction, that of sex. It has been said that Christianity and Buddhism are the only religions of gentleness and feminine virtue, and that these consequently have attracted women devotees. We for ourselves know that Christianity is the most virile force that exists, and we may believe that its undeniable attraction for women is rather in its justice than its mercy. In some lands great multitudes of men have been drawn to a feminine representation of Christianity, and it is plain that the instinct of men is to admire gentleness whilst women venerate strength.

The preacher who has to address congregations of men and women together must not only reckon with the differences of reflection and perception which mark severally the capacities of their minds but he must note also their separate moral qualities. The proximate danger of boy and man is self-confidence and presumption, whilst that of girl and woman is self-contempt and despair. The social moralist is aware that these notes dominate the entire character ; a broken man may be encouraged or spurred to pick himself up again whilst a woman without hope can scarcely re-collect herself. But the man of unbroken success in life is in continuous peril and too often is reckless till he has been schooled by misfortune. The preacher must know the need of such dividing of the Word as will speak confidence to womanhood and teach humility and self-restraint to men.

CHAPTER VIII.

THE LIFE OF CONVERSION.

The Eternal Life—The Living Body—The Life of the Body—Life in the Body—Corporate Conviction—Continuous Consciousness—The Mind of Christ—Evolution of St. Paul—Literary Theology—Æsthetic Religion—Christianity not Respectability—Dangerous Alliances—Modern Ignorance of Scripture—Importance of Exposition—Life of Grace—Gradual Conversion—Spiritual not merely Ethical—Fellowship in Grace—Feeding the Flock—Doing the Truth.

THE building of Solomon's Temple prefigured the raising up in the heavens of the Temple not made with hands. The work of preparing the stones was completed in the quarries; and this world is the quarry in which souls are prepared for their place in glory. We need to lay due emphasis upon that aspect of the spiritual life on earth. Men are apt to believe that here they need only to learn a catch-word, or at the best to make a decision. It is true that the great decision must be made, but that decision must be expressed in a life of increasing preparedness for eternity. If we set before ourselves in even the most insufficient terms the nature of the life beyond the grave we shall feel overwhelmed at the thought of the inadequacy of the most devout life upon earth as the preparation for that to which we aspire. Here all our interests and ambitions and satisfactions and happinesses are in matters which do not outlast the mortal life. And in the life beyond all the happinesses and satisfactions are in the matters which we have touched lightly and theoretically and occasionally in the life on earth. Justification by faith is rightly the adjustment of the life of sense to the unseen world. Sin has interrupted the true intercourse between man and God; from that dislocation we are recovered by grace through faith. The Divine power, grace, moves normally through the heart of the man who is adjusted with God, and operates to produce personal holiness. Holiness is the capacity for seeing God, and for entering into the endless life of the blessed.

With this premiss we may go on to note that the preacher has to deal with men not only as individuals but as members of a living Body, when they come within the Ecclesia. The preacher has to address the world; through him the Holy Ghost confutes and convicts of sin and righteousness and judgment. His external ministry arrests, awakens, and attracts those whom it reaches effectively. But the soul so affected is not left where it was found; it is brought into relationship with God and therefore of necessity with all other souls in grace. It becomes a part of the ordinary sphere of the operation of the Holy Ghost. Sin is the solvent, the disintegrating force, the temper of dissension; and He that came to destroy the works of the Devil gathers together in one all the children of God, scattered throughout the world. Human life is not to be thought of as an existence complete within the short interval between the birth and death of any person. It is a continuous course running on through the generations, and widening with the multiplication of the race. In like manner but with intenser solidarity the life of grace is in the Body of the Redeemed; and the Body of the Redeemed is a living Body, growing into the measure and completeness of a perfected humanity which shall in its wholeness reproduce the likeness of Christ. When God formed man His Breath conveyed the gift of life to the physical being which He had made : and at Pentecost the Breath of God, the Holy Spirit, entered into and possessed and animated the body of disciples which Jesus Christ, the Divine Son, had gathered into unity. The corporate life which became theirs by the descent of the Holy Ghost was altogether another and higher life than that of an organized society.

In this connexion we may notice the continuous misconceptions which express themselves in the appeals ordinarily made to religious bodies. However the phrase may run, with the common misuse of sacred words and terms, it will be seen that persons nominally Christian are addressed as patrons and members of benevolent or mutual improvement societies. Their self-respect is flattered or their *esprit de corps* is invoked or their indignation is aroused by some reference to grievances for the most part imaginary. It is plain that the greatly extended use of the word Church in these last few years synchronizes with a strange lack of spiritual perception and spiritual consciousness. The Church of God is not an organization and does not live upon good fellowship or worldly prosperity. It is the Mystical Body of Christ, the Body of which He is the Head ; and consequently its essential character is the heavenly and the spiritual, and its corporate life is derived directly through spiritual intercourse with Him in heaven. That spiritual intercourse is maintained by the Holy Ghost here upon earth, through the junctures and ligaments which relate it healthfully to the Head. The whole Body is nourished and knit together and increases spiritually by grace. Now grace is the distinctive gift and life of the Christian Church; it is the presence and power of God in

man. Man living in the Christian Covenant is partaker of the Divine nature; he is in grace, he is in
Christ, he is justified with God. And as the promises
and privileges of the old Covenant were given to an elect
people and not to persons severally, so the life of grace
is the common life of the Mystical Body. The Paschal
Lamb cannot be eaten without the house.

There are two essentials of the life which the
members share : they are the two influences which
issue from the Incarnation, grace and truth. These
are inseparable from one another. Controversies touching the symbols of orthodoxy have diverted attention
from the necessity of grace, and have at the same time
incidentally expelled grace from the hearts of those who
have allowed the contention to become a quarrel. But
in fact grace and truth are of necessity related to one
another, and as actually as in the physical body breath
and blood are related. Experimentally it will be found
that the devout communicant receives the Gospel of
Redemption with a directness and apprehension otherwise unattained. And in the propagation of the faith
amongst our people it is wise to promote the life of grace
concurrently with advancing instruction ; and it will be
found that this course is not only the practicable way,
but that it secures also that the new-found knowledge
does not inflate and overset the learner.

In many parts of England the work of the ministry in
teaching the faith has been neutralized by the odious
bearing of small groups of nominal disciples, young people of meagre mental equipment. The preacher who
allows himself to be mobbed by four or five such persons
may reckon his public ministry an accomplished failure ;
these are a commentary on his teaching, and a continual
exposition of its worthlessness. They eat up the good

pasture and tread down the residue with their feet. The harm done by this class of persons is incalculable, the number of honest and sincere people repelled by them is immense, the discouragement caused by them to the clergy is heart-breaking. And when such adherents have stultified the clergy in one parish they will move away lightly to some other field of operations. It often happens in a mission that the first two or three persons to approach the missioner compromise or discredit the mission by their evident lack of balance; and similarly every preacher or pastor needs to be careful of the note and character of any set of persons who may stand out as samples of his ministry.

The woman with the issue of blood who came to our Lord for healing had to push her way resolutely through the crowd that thronged Him and yet had no blessing; the palsied man of Capernaum brought by his friends for healing, had to be lowered through the tiling because the crowd blocked the door; Bartimæus by the roadside clamouring for sight was bidden by the apparent followers of Jesus Christ to hold his tongue. A healthy body will not harbour dead matter; what cannot be assimilated is rejected. And no congregation is in spiritual health whilst it retains in conspicuous position any persons who are not receptive of grace and responsive to truth.

It is necessary to teach the positive obligation of fidelity to the fellowship. It need not be argued whether schism is justified in some parish or locality by some temporary ill-condition of things; schism is not permissible in any case, and is a graver offence than that which may seem to be its cause or provocation. It is in the body of the faithful that truth has its home, and grace its full scope. The soul hesitating in matters of faith or beginning to apprehend is supported by the corporate convictions of the Church. The faith itself is not an ancient group of theories repeated age after age; it is the continuous consciousness of the Church. Christ forbade men with fragmentary or incomplete gospels to preach to their fellows, and when He gave command to convert and teach all nations He spoke at once to the whole company of the Apostles. And our teaching must be whole and Catholic; no partial representation, no private restatement will prove sufficient.

Men have scarcely yet imagined what is meant by a complete Christendom. Every tribe and people has some particular gift for mankind; and, higher yet, will adorn the doctrines of our Saviour Christ in some characteristic way. Human life, grace-transformed, represents Christ in His Sacred Humanity; and a whole Christian world will show us Christ in perfections and splendours of character now unimagined. National Christianity then has an admissible meaning. The term is used generally for what is illegitimate, an adaptation of the Gospel to racial weakness or prejudice. The term is admissible when it denotes fidelity in discipleship, exhibited through some national characteristic. And the various social classes have all their values in this respect; for every class has its ill-propensity and its admirable quality. And the Christian prophet has this plain duty in these times: to insist that no one class is without fault, and that none can exist without its fellows. Men are too ready to tolerate their class sin and even to speak of it with jocularity as a badge of their position, but they need to learn that a class sin is of the character of sleeping on duty at a frontier post.

And every person is called to make also a particular

contribution to the full representation of Christ. We are probably getting away from the foolish supposition that slavish imitation of some ancient Christian leader is the surest road to holiness. Every one severally has a vocation and ministry in which to glorify God. Inspiration by the Holy Ghost and not tedious and servile copying of any person however saintly or eminent is the true spring of the soul's advancing life. The new life is the life constantly renewed; it is not lived upon the waning force of a past experience. And in this life there must of necessity be growth and advancement. There is no point reached at which one may rest content with one's self.

The word conversion may be applied to that change of direction in human life which is summed up in the will to do the Will of God; that would be, in the phrase of St. Augustine, the election of God as the object of the soul's love. But the word conversion may have a wider application, and denote that transformation of character which is the momentous process in man which the Holy Ghost effects. Every gift of grace, taken up through conduct into character, contributes towards that change. You may mark it typically in the experience of St. Paul. In the four groups of epistles which we have from his hand our Lord is set forth successively as Judge, Saviour, King and Head. The conception of Christ in His full ministry and relationship to mankind develops significantly as the missionary experience of the Apostle extends.

And St. Paul's conception of himself correspondingly develops; he knows himself increasingly in the light of the Master. Note the order of St. Paul's self-realization. In his first letter, written to the Thessalonians, he claims boldly: " Ye are witnesses and God also how

9 *

holily and justly and unblameably we behaved ourselves amongst you ". The Apostle has made some progress in the way of discipleship when he comes four or five years later to address the Corinthian Christians by letter; to these he writes : " I am the least of the Apostles that am not meet to be called an Apostle, because I persecuted the Church of God ". Another four or five years pass, with many experiences of privation and suffering, and he addresses the Ephesians : " Unto me, who am less than the least of all saints, is this grace given, that I should preach among the Gentiles the unsearchable riches of Christ ". And yet another four or five years pass and St. Paul writes to St. Timothy : " This is a faithful saying and worthy of all acceptation, that Christ Jesus came into the world to save sinners ; of whom I am chief ". The conversion of St. Paul is the typical instance of instantaneous change ; so far as it was instantaneous it was change of will and direction. There is indeed the sudden arrest, the abrupt halt, the quick awakening ; there God is recognized personally and man's life presented in its true light, and there follows the capitulation : " Lord, what wilt Thou have me to do ". But years of service and experience followed, and affliction and renewals of the Holy Ghost were wrought into the tenseness and patience of Paul the aged. Transformation of life must proceed upon redirection of will, that the convert may become the saint.

In the course of this expanding life forms and phrases that support and assist at one time may constrict and paralyse at a later stage. The use of regular and familiar orders of worship is attended by the danger of formalism and unreality ; the preacher must warn himself and deliver the people from the bondage of phrase and the staleness of routine. Whilst studiously avoiding the use of undignified or unworthy language the preacher should forbid himself the employment of any worn theological phrases. Very considerable effect may be produced by the use of paraphrase, and the translation into other terms of the truths and doctrines which have become ineffective in some familiar and unexamined phrases.

But it is necessary to go farther. In this country Christianity suffers from the disadvantage of bondage to the letter; and this arises from two totally separate causes. In the sixteenth century our national Church passed through a critical experience, in which the leaders were careful to retain the vital tradition of Catholic continuity and at the same time they were anxious to secure the attachment of persons with diverse spiritual temperaments. From this it resulted of necessity that forms of words had exaggerated importance. The settled and accepted forms were the precious securities of stability and brotherhood, the only symbols of peace in times of strife and controversy. Later many of our greatest divines have had to meet able and resolute attacks upon our theological position: Jewel, Laud, Waterland, Bull, Butler, Pearson, are names which represent a literature of which we may be justly proud. But we are noting here the disadvantage of too close an identification of religion with literature: and we glance at the second cause to which allusion has been made. Nonconformity in this country has relied much upon the tract and pamphlet. It is sometimes assumed that the distribution of Bibles and Testaments is by itself the propagation of Christianity. When an attempt is made to maintain the common life of a religious community without a settled ministry reliance must be placed upon the services of persons engaged in ordinary daily avocations, and consequently public exercises of devotion are restricted to one day in the week; and at the same time the circulation of printed matter is disproportionately large to supplement the irregularity and insufficiency of doctrinal instruction. In this country to-day we mark both of these defects in popular religion : the services of six days in the week are gravely neglected, and literary forms are unduly valued. Our people are not generally a literary people, and printed forms do not easily and smoothly enter into the common tenor of their lives. Religion expressed in phrases and idioms purely literary may remain an external adjunct, failing to affect or to control the social and domestic life. You cannot make the common populace all philosophers or students : you must not demand classical taste as a necessary condition of religious fervour or sincerity. The preacher has this office : he must bring home the truth to the heart, and relate common worship to daily life.

The revival of romanticism which owed much to Sir Walter Scott has made ecclesiastical forms interesting to many people who care little for spiritual life; and ecclesiology and Church architecture with kindred arts of stained-glass and fresco painting bring to us numbers of people who have never thought seriously of personal union with God through the Incarnation. Let us not be deceived : romanticism is not a theological grace and does not advance spiritual religion. The great public library in Boston (Massachusetts) contains in its entrance hall a magnificent fresco running with continuous story round its walls. The men that built the great library in that Unitarian city wished to depict there the greatest romance of the world, and debated whether they should find it in the story of Ulysses or King Arthur or in the history of Rome, and in the end they set upon their walls the Life and Death and Resurrection of Christ. That is not there as a spiritual influence, to compel the obedience and love of men, but as a beautiful narrative to produce æsthetic admiration. And sometimes the furnishing of our churches and the rendering of our services may leave nothing to be desired in the way of art and music and liturgical accuracy, whilst " the hungry sheep look up and are not fed, But swollen with wind ".

And if the faithful are to be rightly instructed and shepherded in the new life of fellowship it is important that we distinguish also between the merely ethical and the spiritual. The Church is rather a penitentiary than a thrift society. Respectability has been over-rated and has its own rewards apart from all religious considerations. The ordinary politician regards the Church as an organization that supplies moral ballast to the community, with the addition sometimes of ill-distributed relief. But Christian morals are in profound disagreement with the standards of all purely ethical societies. Christian morals rest upon spiritual truth, conform to the Divine standards, and contemplate an eternal consequence. It is not reason that we should leave the Word of God and serve worldly ends, however important these may be for the world's welfare. We must refuse to be diverted from our vocation by literary interests or artistic tastes or social enterprises or ethical projects or eugenics.

Life was never more full of various interests than it is to-day ; the man that is not intent upon a commanding purpose is easily diverted. The Christian preacher needs to know the supreme importance of his work and message or he will be claimed and appropriated by some social cause. Alliances that seem to promise immediate advantage are to be shunned. History shows that where religious leaders have identified their work with some political movement the results however extensive have failed in spiritual character. Moral effects, and social, and political, may legitimately be the outcome of spiritual life, but none of these have the supreme value.

How are the Christian folk to be taught by the preacher? Consider first how great a work has to be done in this matter by the preacher unaided. Anciently in this land mystery and miracle plays made our people commonly conversant with the salient incidents of Old Testament history. And they knew also how to interpret the stories of the Old Testament in the light of the Incarnation. The children were familiar with the history of God's ancient people through themselves assisting in the dramatic representation of the scenes which were taken from the Old Testament Scriptures. And later our people were accustomed to read the Scriptures for themselves, and to gather from Scripture the main part of their thought. Now all that is changed. Where the habit of Bible reading is not directly a part of the personal rule of devotion it has largely ceased to exist. And what is not taught from the pulpit by the preacher may not be assumed as known in this matter. Expository teaching therefore has come to have more importance than ever; it is by exposition that we may recover the interest and attachment of the people to revealed truth.

A course of exposition treating one book of Holy Scripture continuously for a season or a period will generally be valued in a settled congregation. And where it is necessary to treat the ordinary congregation as a mixed multitude, not yet receptive of doctrinal instruction, some specific occasions should be made for expository teaching.   It will soon be discovered that here is a power of attraction of unsuspected worth.   The catch-title and sensational interrogation which are placarded at the doors of some places of religious profession are evidence of failure in the wholesome ministry of God's Word.   Exposition will attract thinking people, and will stimulate right thought, and will nourish spiritual life.   And expository teaching will keep the preacher always a student, and will retain his own personal interest in the Word which he has to expound.

It is in the diffusion of exposition that the common mind of the Church is formed and becomes coherent. The Kingdom of God upon earth holds the Gospel of the Kingdom.   That was the theme of our Lord's preaching constantly.   He set before men not only as an ideal but as an actuality a society in which God is Sovereign and goodness supreme wealth.   That society, that Kingdom, is the fellowship of the Redeemed here and now; it is not a future state in which men are to find their reward. Here and now the man becomes an integral part of that society; and membership etymologically denotes share in the social life.   The social life of the Church is the necessary spiritual nourishment of every member. None can live in the fellowship without truth and grace.   It is to the Scriptures that the preacher must turn if he would build up healthy belief and stronger conviction.   From the Scriptures he will derive for his people doctrinal instruction: he will help them by the guidance of the Scriptures into the temper of worship: he will encourage by its illuminations the soul's pilgrimage towards heaven.

Conversion is the trend of the life of the disciple

towards personal holiness; it is the gradual occupation
of the whole being by grace. St. Bernard teaches us
that the grace of adoption, conferred in Baptism, needs
to be fertilized by personal faith in subsequent life.
That kindling of spiritual consciousness which disposes
the will to co-operate with the Will of God is the soul
rising to its birthright. There is then interaction between the Holy Ghost and the soul awakened : and
thenceforward conference with the Holy Ghost must light
the way, consent with the Holy Ghost must guide the
will, and co-operation with the Holy Ghost must make
the growth of the new self. As in the reception of spiritual
truth the whole being is involved, will, intellect and affection, so in the new life of transforming character all must
be possessed by Christ. One may have the will to live
holily, justly, and unblameably, long before one can love
one's enemies. The will reconciled to God is the healing of the wound of sin which Satan has inflicted on
the heart, and man is convalescent in grace. In the
processes of recovery which move toward perfection
all the apostolic admonitions have their place—bring
into captivity every thought to the obedience of Christ
—whatsoever things are true, honest, just, pure, lovely,
think on these things—covet earnestly the best gifts,
faith, hope and charity. Gradually by the power of
the indwelling Comforter intellect and affection, thought
and feeling, become so sanctified as to make heavenly
mindedness the prevailing consciousness and sustenance of the disciple.

What part has the preacher in this experience of increasing conversion, this movement of obedience to the
heavenly vision ? He has to keep before the soul in all
its movement high and noble conceptions of God. No
other teaching about religion will serve in place of this;

here is the vital note of truth. The various popular misrepresentations of the Gospel are due to so many mistakes touching the Nature of God : and equally the defects which mar the spiritual lives of men are the outcome of personal misapprehensions of the Divine Character. The most direct way to the enrichment of human morality is the fuller exposition of Deity. Of necessity a man's conception of God is the foundation of his own moral character. God made man in His Own Image and Likeness : there is still no other ideal for man in place of that. But man is prone to think God altogether such an one as himself, and with that there comes the total collapse of ideal, and the nerve of morality is cut. The preacher must inspire the people with reverence and godly fear, that temper which recognizes the facts of God's greatness and goodness and man's unworthiness. He must exalt God, and cause it that confidence in God's Love does not induce a neglect of exact duty, or promote self-satisfaction.

Consider how hopelessly the majority of our people, even the best and kindliest, would be put to it if they were asked to state in their own words and without the quotation of any text, what God is. If it is true, as it surely is, that every man's personal character reflects his personal conception of God, it is of the first importance that we teach in such wise as to enable every man that hears us to see also the Lord sitting upon the throne, high and lifted up. If grace is the life principle by which the soul grows when justified with God, the knowledge of God Himself is the motive of the soul in grace.

The life of the disciple is in the fellowship of the faithful, and this fellowship is constituted in Christ. Another name for fellowship is communion ; and this

word may help us to realize some of the notes of fellowship.   The soul lives by the life derived from God, and
this supernatural life the soul shares with all others
that live in Christ.   The obligation of mutual service
will follow after; the recognition of the common life is
the first necessity, and with that the acknowledgment
of mutual dependence.   It will need constant and patient
teaching if our people are to be recovered from the
materialism of these times, the instinctive reckoning of
worldly profits, and the obsequious deference offered to
wealth.   We have to throw another emphasis upon life,
to insist upon the reality of the unseen, the closeness
of spiritual kinship, and the prime importance of spiritual gifts.

This requires a true sense of proportion in ourselves,
and we need to form the habit of spiritual discernment.
It was said of a preacher, evidently urgent to deliver his
Gospel, that he spoke as a dying man to dying men; it
is for every one of us to speak as a living man to men
alive spiritually.   St. Paul teaches us that the Christian
man looks on the unseen which is the eternal; and we
have to form and encourage in ourselves and in others
the instinct of reckoning the things of this life as rela-
tively unimportant.   We must constantly advert to unseen and spiritual causes of things on the surface of
human experience; we must know that however far
back we may trace natural law it rests yet farther back
upon Divine volition.   We must accustom ourselves to
interpret all the observed incidents of life as manifesta-
tions of Divine wisdom and Divine justice and Divine
purpose.   We must school ourselves to patience by
marking the certain emergence of good from evil and
the sure triumph of righteousness and justice since the
Lord of all the earth will do right.   We must trace with

filial gratitude the marvellous ways in which God has vindicated His own, again and again bringing His people out of bondage and opening for them ways through the sea. We must claim all the sciences as notes in the song of praise of the one God, Maker of heaven and earth, and of all things visible and invisible.

We may carry our literary interests into the remotest provinces of human learning, only remembering always the charge laid upon us at our ordination that we apply ourselves wholly to this one thing and draw all our cares and studies this way. No other part of the preacher's work is weightier than this, the guidance and feeding of the spiritual mind of those who are within. If the preacher is wanting here, converts will fall away, and those who have been awakened will perish in the wilderness. In the endeavour to meet the needs of those who have made some advance in the life of grace the most frequent mistake is the lack of simplicity in preaching. It is not necessary to offer to these abstruse theological discussions; the highest and profoundest teaching of the faith is in the clearest and simplest narrative of the Gospel. The epistles have their relative worth as they help us to know and apply the teachings which are in the Word Himself. The preacher will be conscious of the support and endorsement which is given to his testimony by the ready faith of those in the discipleship; their spiritual sympathy and witness give an effective commendation to his ministry. They are the epistle of God written by the Holy Ghost and known of all men. Whilst the preacher is the minister of God with the message from God he is also the voice of the fellowship, adding to the announcement of God's message the verification of human experience.

The preacher is the minister of truth. He has to offer the truth with its attractive influences to the world. And when men realize their need of the word of truth, and recognize their necessary relation to it, the preacher must help them to know it as the correction and rectification of human life. As the spiritual life deepens the soul in grace becomes more and more susceptible of the truth and responsive to its claim. This is the phrase of St. John the Divine; he speaks of those who walk in darkness and "do not the truth". "Doing the truth" is the new life of man re-created in Christ; it is conformity to the Divine Will, and faithful fulfilment of God's purpose in the creation of man. In this new life the ministry of the Word directly nourishes the soul.

And the preacher must reckon with the spiritual appetite of those who feed upon the Word of God. Everywhere may be found some who by immediate intuition derive direct intimations from the Holy Spirit by means of the Word; for the text of Scripture is in some sense sacramental. In various ages of the Christian Church different methods of interpretation of Scripture have obtained; so much we may learn from history. But we may also learn from experience that all these methods co-exist to-day amongst our people, and the reading or preaching of the Word is now as on the day of Pentecost heard by every man in his own tongue. Mysticism, discredited when it is misunderstood, is that spiritual faculty of the devout soul which apprehends Divine truth at first hand and consequently at one glance sees the heavenly light in the lantern of phrase or text. The preacher who desires to strengthen the life of the Church will not be constantly exhorting people to practical action. Whilst he will not undervalue the evidence of sincerity which good works may offer he will aim rather at deeper and more lasting results. In all his ministry he will desire to speak to those who feed upon the Word and become themselves evidences of its transforming power.

CHAPTER IX.

INSTRUCTION IN RELIGIOUS KNOWLEDGE.

The Church at the Restoration—Reckoning with Arrears—Sponsors and Godparents—Guilds of Sponsors—Witnesses of Baptism of Adults—Sunday School Teachers—Teachers Licensed by the Bishop—Bible Classes—French Conferences—Parish Conventions—Sectional Services—Devotional Books—Family Charters—Family Prayers—Home Religion.

THE preface of the Prayer Book alludes to a condition of common life in England which necessitated the addition to our Prayer Book in 1661 of a form of Baptism for those of Riper Years. The growth of Ana-baptism through the licentiousness of the times made this necessary. A book published in 1665—Grant's " Obstructions on the Bills of Mortality "—contains the statement that not half the people of England between 1650 and 1660 were convinced of the need of Baptism. The infidelity and profligacy which marked the reign of Charles II were not only the inevitable reaction from the melancholy austerity of Puritanism : they were the natural product of a population left without Baptismal grace. The Church at the Restoration took up definitely and courageously the task of re-Christianizing England. We have now to reckon with arrears almost as appalling as those of the seventeenth century. The necessary domestic tradition of religion is well-nigh lost. Whilst it is true that a prejudice against some particular belief

may still pass from parents to children, unhappily a disposition towards positive belief is rarely carried from generation to generation.   We must never abate the claim
which the Church makes on the Christian parents. Other
means and other influences must supplement, and not
supplant, the home and the parent.

The appointment of godparents is a very ancient provision of the Church to secure the spiritual care of the
child in case of the death of the parents.   Anciently in
England, as now in the Greek and Latin Churches, only
one sponsor was required : this one always received the
newly baptized infant from the hands of the priest, and
represented the spiritual kindred into which Baptism
brought the infant.   In England the Church, taught by
the religious disasters of the period of Oliver Cromwell,
made the rule that requires three sponsors besides the
parents. An alteration in our Canon, added by the Con-
vocation of Canterbury in 1865, now makes it permissible
for parents to act as sponsors for their children.   This
brings us back virtually to the earlier rule that one
other person, of the same sex as the infant, shall stand
with the parents at the font.   And now we must all
acknowledge that this institution, so wise in its purpose
and so expressive of a right regard for the little ones
whose angels do always behold the Face of the Father,
has fallen into lamentable decay. Rightly used it had
given continuous support to the domestic tradition of
religious instruction : it has become little more than a
social compliment and pretty custom.

It is proposed by some persons to revive sponsor-
ship by enrolling suitable persons in parochial guilds of
sponsors.   In all our great cities the parish priests are
frequently asked to baptize children for whose religious
upbringing there can be scarcely any security.   The

poor mother alone, and sometimes half-drunken, brings her child to church.   No condition can be required, no stipulation made ; the dilemma is plain, to give Baptism with all its awful solemnities to a foundling that emerges from the unknown and recedes into the unknown, or to refuse Baptism.   Of the two alternatives the second is worse; and Baptism is given, usually with some intention of the priest to take up this new charge personally.   Probably no one would undertake deliberately to justify our present disorder in the administration of Baptism ; but again the default is on the part of the laity, and it is the neglect of their duty by nominally Christian parents which makes the work of the clergy so difficult.   The guilds of sponsors may be of some help to us; but the measure of their service and worth will naturally depend upon their constitution. If persons are to be enrolled as the godparents of any poor children who, for lack of other sponsors, may be assigned to them by the parish priest, it is evident that these are to have a calling and status entirely different from that of the good-natured district visitor. These godparents must be eminently people of devotion and prayer; they must be chosen without regard for worldly station or fortune.   If we might secure a due continuity for a devotional society of this character in a parish perhaps in time we might revive the Agape. And a society of sponsors would perhaps advance the recovery of spiritual discipline, and prompt the recognition of the Church as a penitential body.

As the angels have their ministry in continual guardianship of the soul till it reaches the state of the blessed, so sponsors have a duty of continuous watchfulness till the baptized has passed into the full membership and communion of the Church.   Therefore godparents are appointed even for one who is baptized as an adult, though the catechumen can speak for himself.   These godparents are not sponsors but witnesses; and they are to be witnesses also of the subsequent Confirmation of the newly baptized.   Their fellowship is the support of the convert and an encouragement to him to advance with confidence.   Even where there are not yet organized societies of sponsors it is to be desired that an adult person at Baptism be met at the font by a small company of men or women as the case may require, representative of the faithful.   The newly baptized person should be assured of the kindly comradeship of those to whom he is now related; he must realize the kingdom of grace.

Before we devise new things it is well to reckon over our present possessions.   In the course of the past two centuries we have gradually enlisted in the service of the Church a great army of Sunday school teachers. We do not under-rate their worth when we note the serious limitations which fetter their service.   In the Canons of 1604 it is appointed that schoolmasters are to be licensed by the Bishop of the diocese, and further that all schoolmasters shall teach the Catechism and Holy Scripture to the children.   It may be generally taken that the Archbishop's certificate, awarded to the students in our training colleges on examination, is a modern equivalent in practice for the episcopal licence. The Sunday school teacher has never held so regular or definite a position.   It is not necessary to say that the circumstances of the ordinary Sunday school assembly seriously hamper instruction.   The children are more stiffly clothed, and are instinctively aware of the lack of regular discipline; and the teachers, though often capable and very diligent, have not had

10 *

technical training. It is not desirable that day school teachers be invited to take up Sunday school work.

But if the difficulties of Sunday school teaching are great and many there is the more need of certain securities of attainable efficiency. First, every teacher should be—is it necessary to say?—in the life of grace and fidelity. It may be assumed that there is willingness to teach and correspondingly a readiness to learn and to co-operate with all others who are teaching in the same school or group. As the parish priest is responsible for the whole flock it is his duty to appoint and draw out a scheme of instruction so that all the children in the varying degrees of capacity may be receiving the same teaching. He should further undertake the work of teaching the teachers at the close of the Sunday schools on Sunday afternoon. This teaching will be all the more effective if it is concurrent with a printed course on the subjects chosen for the year. For instance, the Gospel of St. Mark may be taken as the continuous subject for one year; a small manual of St. Mark is named for adoption, and the subject-matter divided into forty sections. The great festivals and special occasions complete the number of the Sundays. One of the forty sections is then treated in the Sunday afternoon class for teachers; and that lesson is given by the teachers severally on the Sunday following. On the first Sunday in the month at the children's service the children are catechized on the lessons which they have so received. By this method two great principles are secured: first the teaching is definite and systematic, and secondly it is harmoniously and effectively propagated. In drawing up the scheme of instruction it is well to consider what effect ought to be produced. It is impossible even if it were desirable that the children should learn sections of Scripture history and lists of events, of miracles or of parables. Our best school-masters in the elementary day schools are aware that the children almost invariably forget two-thirds of what they have learned at school within three years of leaving school. In our Sunday schools the impression that is made upon the children is probably still more shallow. It is possible to create lastingly nothing but a distaste for the Scriptures, and a disregard of religious instruction.

Day schools and Sunday schools alike should bear some part in the preparing of the children for full and continuous membership in the Church. We should de-sire to teach the children in the schools not what they must learn but how to learn all their lives through. The main principles of the Christian faith, the Divinity of our Lord, the Presence and Work of the Holy Ghost, the Divine Mission of the Church, the need of sacra-mental grace, the nature of penitence, are the vital sub-ject-matter; in acquiring this the child is preparing for Confirmation, for the life of Communion, and the life beyond the grave. When the child has left school there should be no doubt in the child's mind as to the duty of fidelity to the Church. But our Army chaplains inform us that of the whole number of recruits that enlist even from our country parishes comparatively few are con-firmed, and rarely one knows even the theory of his re-ligion. And our colonial clergy assure us that the emigrants that leave England for Canada or New Zea-land or Australia are almost entirely ignorant of the principles of Christianity or the duty of paying for the maintenance of worship. The clergy are responsible for the religious instruction of their people; and yet it is possible for a person to grow up from infancy to man-hood in a country parish furnished with Church schools and to live and die without any definite knowledge of the Creed of the Church.

You may find usually in the home of a Tyrolese peasant a large illuminated card which is hung in a place of honour. It is the family charter, and is somewhat akin to our erstwhile family Bible. The family charter contains in its regular spaces the names of the father and mother of the family with the date of their wedding, and records the Baptism and Confirmation and first Communion of the children in the order of their age. It has also space for the last Communion or death of any member of the household. And all its records are set within a framework of doctrinal statements, eminently clear and preciously Christian. It begins with the dedication of the home to the glory of the Father and of the Son and of the Holy Ghost; and it ends with the invocation of the Blessed Comforter, the Spirit of peace and love and patience, Who will perform His great Work till the day of Jesus Christ. We have lost the family Bible; we might well adopt the family charter. Its place in the house or the cottage would be of great value in these days. And if we can adopt in this country the family charter we may perhaps add to it in some places the rule of general prayer at a concerted moment every morning and every evening. It has been found possible to institute this in some parishes, and to accustom the people to make their private or their family prayers when one of the church bells rings out. By such means the whole people may be moved to common devotion and mutual intercession, and the spirit of religion maintained as the most persistent and penetrative force in the community.

In the home life itself the ordinary customs should be practical expressions of the teachings of Christianity;

the courtesy of one to another, the chivalry that moves the boys to wait upon their sisters, the principles of unselfishness and especially that considerateness which asks as little as possible of the personal service of others, best exemplify the lessons of the Incarnation. The enactment of the old Covenant was, Thou shalt teach these words diligently unto thy children, and shalt talk of them when thou sittest in thine house, when thou walkest by the way, and when thou liest down, and when thou risest up; thou shalt bind them for a sign upon thine hand, and they shall be as frontlets before thine eyes, and thou shalt write them upon the posts of thine house and on thy gates. The Hebrews have maintained the letter of this law; we must maintain its spirit. They in all their dwellings to-day fasten the brief inscriptions of the law in the wooden frame of their doors; we must apply the teachings of the Gospel to all our going and coming, the manner of our intercourse with our fellowmen, the motive and purpose of our departure or return.

In the larger family life of the parish there are other opportunities for religious instruction. The common term, Bible Class, covers a vast number of assemblies and societies of different characters and of various values. These may be for men or for women, but rarely for both men and women together. The method to be followed in a Bible Class must be determined by the mental ability of the members. A class of educated people might make a study of one book of the Scriptures exhaustively; whilst another class of less intellectual capacity would find that method tedious and wearisome. But in general a class ought to be taught from the four books of the Gospel outwards, to know the salient meaning of the several Old Testament stories as they foretell the Redeemer, and to understand the Epistles as exhortations based upon the Divine Assumption of our nature, and addressed to those in the fellowship. Subjects and themes rather than passages of Scripture should form the course of Bible Class instruction.

And immediately arising out of this is the consideration of special services in church for men and for women. We all acquiesce in a condition of things that we find in possession; but if we hold or allow these sectional services we may yet retain a conviction that they are not to be desired or encouraged. The congregation of the whole parish is a spiritual entity, having definite character and spiritual constitution. Groups arbitrarily taken lack the balance and complement that they should find in the general assembly. It is better for a man to go to church with his wife and children, better for the woman to go as the wife and mother, better for the children to go with their mother and father, than for any of these to go separately to services for men or for women or for children. And further, the arrangement and announcement of these sectional services will generally exaggerate the note of sex, which is not by any means to be desired. When a word has to be said to the fathers or to the mothers particularly it will be heard with more attention, and perhaps better remembered, if it comes as a parenthesis in a general parish sermon. Is it necessary to say that such a word must never be harsh or corrective? it should be rather so persuasive that those to whom it is spoken feel honoured by the passing courtesy.

But if we hesitate as to the sectional services there can be no doubt that Lent and Advent are to be used for such courses and means of instruction. We generally fail to claim the liberty that is ours to use our churches for really popular assemblies. It is permissible to add to the daily services, which are of obligation, occasions of less formality; as it is common to hold in some central city churches midday services, which consist of two or three collects and a hymn followed by an address, so in any parish church, at some other hour of the day, instructions may be given. In some parts of the French Church a course of *Conférences* will be given during Lent at some appointed hour week by week. The subject of the course is announced beforehand and people are interested and urged to regular attendance. In the English Church something of this kind has been attempted, with at least promising results. It is not important how such a course is named so long only as the people are enabled to distinguish what is proposed from other methods of which they may be tired. Let us call such a series of addresses a parish Convention, and announce widely beforehand that it will be held on a certain night weekly throughout Lent. Let the people know that the Convention will meet at eight and disperse at nine punctually. And let there be a Convention hymn paper containing five or six hymns very plainly printed; the tunes of these hymns must be good and rhythmical. And let there be some means of registering the attendance—a linen-backed card of membership to be date-stamped at the church door, or a large card of memorial, to be gradually filled up at home by the printed gummed slips of doctrinal notes distributed at the end of the address. A parish Convention may bring together hundreds of persons who are not seen at church on Sundays, for they " have no clothes " or they do not know " how to turn the book "; and this method will ensure attendance so regular as to maintain 95 per cent of the total throughout Lent.

Experience justifies us in believing that a Lent Convention pours systematic instruction into the hearts of the people with a directness and completeness otherwise unattained. Year after year as Lent approaches the members of former Conventions speak to their neighbours and engage their interest for the coming opportunity: and it is possible to make the course of addresses in the Convention to be of any desirable character, on the Commandments, or the Creed, or social life, or home duties, or prayer and Sacraments. The preacher should speak with the personal note of pastoral insight and parochial experience. The Lord's Prayer and a hymn preceding the address, the second hymn and the blessing following it, will leave about fifty minutes for the address itself.

Twenty years ago a great Franciscan preacher in the north of Italy gave courses of sermons and instructions in Florence and Milan and Rome. These were singularly forcible and effective. And the congregations that listened to him with sustained attention were enormous, and were composed of persons of all classes, but chiefly of the artisan class. And this is the more notable because his method was not such as would be thought to be likely to attract people not accustomed to study. This preacher began, as soon as he reached the pulpit, by making a short evangelical address to the people; this would probably induce a sympathetic disposition in his hearers. Then he sat down in the pulpit for a few moments, whilst the congregation waited with great expectancy. Rising again to his feet and looking directly before him he repeated clearly and impassively without inflection of voice a brief summary of the doctrinal addresses of previous days, taking up in that way the thread of his mission course. And then with scarcely a pause he announced the subject or passage of Scripture upon which he would now preach, and in a moment flung himself into the great oration of the day. This carried every one along with strained eagerness, and every point, emphasized with eloquence and vivacity, was seized by the whole congregation with an irrepressible murmur of sympathy and conviction. And then suddenly the torrent stayed, and the preacher recovered himself into immediate restraint and quietly recited the doctrinal summary of this new oration. That method had certain evident values. It evoked sympathy and moved people to spiritual receptivity; it compelled attention, it provoked expectation, and assisted memory; it gathered the lessons that men desired to retain into proportionate and balanced definition. It gave the conclusions of the preacher to men who approved as they heard it the process of reasoning which led up to those conclusions.

In some parts of France another method has been used which is not for us available, as the method of the Italian preacher is. The conductor of the *Conférence* ascends the pulpit and makes a short address to the people on some Christian grace. As he proceeds to doctrine he is interrupted by some outcry at the farther end of the church; and presently it is apparent that the preacher is forced into open controversy and thrown upon the defence of his doctrines by a sceptical stranger. It is all a rehearsed piece, and the stranger is a friend from a seminary or a distant parish, who has the task of making a foil for the clearer display of the Gospel of the preacher. Usually the intruder is gradually beaten down in the argument; and sometimes he dramatically professes conversion and kneels to receive the preacher's blessing.

This method cannot be recommended for use in England ; it is unreal and histrionic. But even then it may teach us by suggestion. The preacher ought to know what is passing in the minds of his hearers, and what they would say at the worst if they were allowed to speak their doubts or answer his assertions. Ordinarily the preacher suffers the disadvantage of having to state his case as against a silent adversary, and on the other side there are no mistakes or admissions or palpably weak arguments. Sometimes an attempt is made to secure the expression of the doubts or difficulties of people by placing in the church a letter-box for the reception of notes and questions with which the preacher may deal on some appointed occasion. And this plan is not without good results ; but it will be found that generally the questions asked are not in reference to spiritual things, but rather relate to ecclesiastical politics, to fables and endless genealogies, to foolish and unlearned contentions which gender strifes. One question in ten may lead out some spiritual lesson ; but the writers of the other nine questions will advertise it widely that their inquiries have remained unanswered from ignorance or cowardice.

In England during the past fifty years missions of various kinds have been preached. At the beginning of the movement in this country the missioners naturally followed so far as they could the plan of John Wesley, and preached as he preached repentance as a new birth unto righteousness. Very soon however the character of missions became more formal and scholastic ; until gradually the edification of the faithful was rather sought than the conversion of sinners. A mission entirely devoted to the teaching of doctrine may more fitly be regarded as a parochial retreat, without the advantages of discipline.

But there has been recently a well-defined return to the truer conception of a mission which formerly obtained. And now missioners very generally, whilst they may have various classes or sectional meetings in the course of the day, concentrate themselves upon the mission service at night as the great opportunity. At this service there are two addresses, the first evangelical and the second doctrinal. There should be no long or marked break between these addresses ; a hymn may be sung kneeling, and fittest for the occasion is some hymn of the Holy Spirit. The first of the two addresses should move the people and win their assent ; the second should teach them sympathetically and definitely.

In the short period of a mission the people as a whole should be brought into a new attitude towards religious truth, and old prejudices should be entirely dissolved. In this operation the missioner will avoid the use of contentious language ; he will denounce no formal expression of religious belief ; he will present truth so attractively and positively as to dissipate error or falsehood. The second address ought never to be tedious or long. It may begin with a short recital of the doctrinal lessons of previous days ; and sometimes it is well to let the whole congregation recite these summaries together, and clearly. It is of assistance to the memory of the people if these doctrinal summaries are put into verse ; every night a new verse is added carrying the new lesson.   In that case the instruction begins with the recitation of all the verses of preceding nights, and ends with the verse then learned. At the end of the mission the verses may be printed and given to those who desire to have them. This method has the advantage also of keeping continuous and proportioned the theme throughout the course. The missioner ought to be prepared to vary the direction of his instruction as may be necessary, and correspondingly to make new verses to carry these lessons; in this way the method does not become rigid or intractable. It is true that some missioners prefer to dismiss the principal congregation after the first address, and to deal with those who elect to remain in smaller numbers. But if it be asked what determines some to remain whilst others depart from the church it is probable the answer must be that it is chiefly a matter of convenience. If you suggest to a number of people that they may prefer to leave they will take a light view of the position; it is very improbable that many will feel the urgency of the matter. And a hundred persons remaining after six hundred have left are at once chilled and scattered; there is no cohesion, no common conviction, no intense belief. Missioners who use this method desire to make the more direct appeal to those who seem to have the will-to-believe; but the method does not secure that the more spiritually minded are retained for the second address.

But the preacher is able to rely upon another aid, of secondary value—the circulation of doctrinal and devotional books amongst the people. This can never be a right substitute for oral instruction, but it may afford support and corroboration to the spoken word. Books should be named by the preacher for those who would follow up with more detail any particular line of thought, for the soul's health. And those who are in grace should be advised to set up, on however small a scale, a shelf of devotional works, and to gradually form a little library on the foundation of Jeremy Taylor, and Bull, and Law, and Wilson, and Ken. There has been in recent years a marked decline in the matter of devotional reading; though it may be the total number of little manuals of prayer has increased. Such books as "The Institution of a Christian Man" and "The Whole Duty of Man" had continuous circulation and repeated editions in the sixteenth and eighteenth centuries. They were not only books of prayer; they contained also spiritual instruction. Persons who used these books habitually were helped to a right understanding of Holy Scripture, and a true application of its principles to human life. It is a good thing to encourage the sale of carefully chosen books at some shop conveniently near the church; and for many reasons this business should be carried on through the ordinary channels of book-selling. It will be easy to find a tradesman glad to accept guidance in the selection of books, and notice of those which may be presently recommended for common use.

In all these ways what must be sought is this—the promotion of the life of grace in the soul. We are not to seek as an end the literary or intellectual advancement of the people, or to make them well informed or devoted partisans. There has been constantly in England an unreasoning hesitancy, amounting almost to a neutrality, in matters of faith. When the Long Parliament discussed an order of the House to forbid bowing at the Sacred Name one of their number exclaimed, "Was it ever heard that any other people forbade too great a reverence for their God?" His astonishment was justified, and again and again in our history we have had extraordinary symptoms of wariness or suspicion for the religion which we profess. Episcopacy, for instance, was suppressed and penalized in Scotland at the end of the seventeenth century by an English Parliament of Episcopalians; and Presbyterianism was set up and established by men who professed devotion to One,

Catholic and Apostolic Church.   This is in great measure due to the common supposition that religion may
be taken in quantities, and that Christianity has no
vertebrate structure.   A volume of sermons recently
published by the retired head-master of a public school
illustrates this conveniently.   The sermons are well
written essays on manliness and patriotism and honour ;
they contain no reference to the divine way of salvation
or to the existence of the Mystical Body of Christ.
Teaching of that kind would not necessarily change if
Moslemism replaced Christianity in our land; and it is
entirely worthless in the direct formation of Christian
character.   From such influences our educated classes
pass out to positions of rule and administration at home
and abroad, and the results spiritually are calamitous.
We must recover the proved methods of the early Church,
the proclamation of the Gospel of the Kingdom, the
withholding of membership from the irresolute, the discipline of them that are within.   We must refuse to
compromise with what is called undenominationalism,
and we must be prepared to suffer for our principles.

Apparently some of our ecclesiastical leaders are
willing to provide for a considerable proportion of our
population a religion that cannot be honestly identified
with Christianity.   The appointment of Scripture-readers
to do pastoral work in our great towns, and the provision
of mission rooms for services on Sunday evenings are an
open profession of the needlessness of the Sacraments.
If these things were first tried as an experiment, with
the purpose of opening the way of approach to the
Church for the working-classes, their complete failure in
this matter would justify the immediate abandonment of
the system.   But now we have growing up in our big
cities and nominally under the sanction of the Church

groups of persons who meet only in mission rooms and are content with exhortations from a Scripture-reader for their whole spiritual food. The publication in the eighteenth century of a book which explained Christianity as a natural system, without mysteries and without miracles, was understood rightly to be an attack upon its Divine authenticity; and the offer to the poor of a form of religion that ignores the Sacraments is a cynical denial of the truth of the Gospel. The preacher who would take heed to the flock and feed the Church of God which He has purchased with His Own Blood must first learn for himself the distinctive notes of Christianity. He must know it as the revelation of God through the eternal Son; he must realize it as that calling to which all life must be a response. And he must teach that it is only by the continuous help of the Holy Ghost that fallen man can rise and respond.

CHAPTER X.

CHRISTIAN DUTY.

The Christian Profession—The Baptismal Contract—Conditional Salvation—Obligation of Learning—Greek, Latin and Anglican—Indifference to Truth—The Call to Worship—The Social Witness—Ministry and Vocation—The Duty of Teaching—Preparation of the Preacher—(1) Day Schools, (2) Meditations, (3) Analysis and Study, (4) Parochial Experience.

IT is evident that the man in grace is under an obligation to make a public profession of Christianity. This lesson is taught in ways innumerable in the Gospel. The lepers cleansed are bidden to show themselves to the priests, and to offer the public testimony that Moses commanded; even the woman healed secretly of an issue of blood is called to give her witness before all the people. And all through the ages this duty has been laid upon the newly converted; in some way they must make their profession. The change of name on the Baptism of a convert was partly for this purpose; it marked openly the change of status and citizenship, the admission into the fellowship of grace. Public profession helps the convert himself; it is that first step which costs. And after that step is taken, and the break with the past is complete, the way lies open. But it is chiefly as a testimony unto others that public profession is important. There is no more telling evidence for the worth and power of Christianity than the quiet and constant affirmation of those who set to their seal that God is true.

The position of the disciple in Christ is one of covenant union with God; and a covenant is necessarily two-sided. We must confess Him in this life, and He will confess us hereafter; if we deny Him, He also will deny us. There has never been any way of union with God but through Covenant. The happiness of Eden was based upon Covenant, and all the blessings of Patriarchs were in Covenants given by God and accepted by men. The baptismal contract is a Covenant in express terms. The Church has not arbitrarily devised for us its duties and obligations; they are the necessary conditions of salvation involved in union with God. The Church helps us by setting out plainly the terms upon which alone man can live in a state of salvation. They are three, and they arise out of the Love of God. The Love of God requires that man shall cease from enmity against Him, and shall recover from the poison which Satan has introduced into human nature; the Love of God requires that man shall be drawn into the Divine confidence and brought into understanding with God; the Love of God cannot be satisfied unless man co-operates with God and walks in agreement with Him. These three demands of Love are set out in what we commonly call the baptismal vows; they are the vows of renunciation, faith and obedience. Every baptized person is under these obligations as the prior engagements of life; that is to say no other promise subsequently made that conflicts with these is morally valid or binding. The conventions of society and the duties of honour as they are called are of no weight as against these. And the fulfilment of these vows is the absolutely necessary condition of

11 *

final salvation.   Baptism itself is admission into a state
in which there must be continuance and endurance to
the end; the three vows mark the essential qualities of
that state of endurance.

It is remarkable that in different parts of the Church
the Christian duty is variously apprehended.   The
Greeks conceive of religion as theology, and are jealous
of precision of phrase and exactness of definition.   The
Latins regard personal devotion and worship as the
one thing to be secured at any cost.   The English
reckon conduct to be the only essential thing, the true
aim of all religious observances.   We need not weigh
the question and ask which of the three is the highest
conception or truest recognition of Christianity.   We
ought rather to note the dependence of every one of
these three upon the two others if a true measure of
Christian fidelity is to be attained.   And we need most
to warn ourselves against our proximate danger, the
supposition that philanthropy or good nature can suffice
as a title to heaven or can constitute a claim to be called
Christian.   The strictly correct order of these three
things is knowledge, worship, conduct; it is the order
of the wise men of the East.   When they were come
into the house, they saw the young Child with Mary
His Mother, and they fell down and worshipped Him,
and when they had opened their treasures they offered
Him gifts.

Too often a complaisant philanthropy is held to be a
sufficient discharge of one's duty to God; St. Paul was
eager to say, We seek not yours but you.   The man who
refuses without consideration the doctrines of Christ, and
assumes the name of Christian because he is good-
natured or kind-hearted is in an insolent attitude towards
God.   The Church ought to refuse the gifts of such

persons, and insist that all must begin with the fear of the Lord and humble themselves under His mighty Hand. The utter failure of any other order is exemplified with notorious frequency in our own experience ; for it constantly happens that a man having made a great fortune in business, retires to leisure and adopts a position of social eminence. He becomes the patron of many charities and gives freely to many worthy objects ; but his personal religion is rather worse than it was in his former state when he worked at his trade and made no pretence of being better than his neighbours. In some great towns of the north of England Unitarianism, which has there no vertebrate theology, is the natural pose of such persons in the matter of religion. As a false religion is worse than none, so conduct that is not based upon spiritual knowledge and worship is no acceptable service of God.

If we approach conduct through knowledge and worship we shall probably understand Christian duty ; for in that case it will be informed by our knowledge of God, and inspired by our devotion to Him. But it is here that we are lacking. We have no such zeal for doctrinal knowledge as may be found amongst the Greeks, nor such instinctive addiction to worship as may be found amongst the Latins. And here the preacher may find a great demand upon his ministry ; for he must not simply meet a real need, he must first help his people to know their need in this matter, he has to create an appetite for divine learning, and to compel his people to recognize their obligation in reference to spiritual truth.

It is commonly assumed that every man innately or intuitively knows all that he needs to know of the spiritual, whereas in fact the natural contents of man in this matter are an appetite and not a food. We need to be taught from without, and the second of our baptismal vows binds us solemnly to learn all the articles of the Christian faith.   It is amazing that intelligent people can lightly disregard this solemn obligation, and are content to live out their lives without facing the question, " When and where did you learn your faith ? "   The reason for this negligence is not far to seek ; it is assumed very commonly that nothing is certainly true, and that one religion is as good as another.   If, for instance, missionary work is discussed informally in a casual group of nominal Christians it will be certainly suggested by some that Buddhism is good enough for Indians, and Islamism for Turks and Arabs, and even further that Islamism is better than Christianity for the African races.   Without following the argument we notice the premiss, that all religions are equally true or false.   The supreme worth of truth is not recognized ; and the question whether Christianity is true is not raised.   Now the baptized person is pledged to hold the truth, to grasp the faith.   And the Christian life is the adornment of the doctrines of our Saviour Christ.

The preacher has to move the people to fidelity and loyalty to revelation ; it is his duty as well as his right to call upon them as persons solemnly pledged to learn and to obey all the articles of the Christian faith.   If he would do this he will find the need of stimulating a true interest in the Holy Scriptures, and a right discernment of the relative values of the books that constitute that collection.   It is a good plan to group for a definite season all pulpit instruction round one of the four books of the Gospel.   In that case the chosen book would be expounded in a course of addresses to the faithful ; texts taken from that book would be

treated in a series of sermons; and at other times,
relative to these texts and sermons, addresses would
be given from parts of the Old Testament books of
history and prophecy, and from the Epistles also.
The idea would be to affirm the Divine Mission of
our Lord and to associate all the teachings of Scripture and all the doctrines of our religion with that
foundation truth. The Creeds ought to be expounded
in this connexion ; and experimentally it will be found
that a short series of addresses on any one of the Creeds
will be followed by the people with intense interest.
There is too often a note of debate or discussion in the
pulpit; our charge is to deliver to people what we have
received, and to commend to them by every means
that we can command the Revelation of God in Christ.
The innumerable divisions of Christians in this country
on doctrinal differences and contentions have been deplorable, but perhaps the fusion of a large number of
bodies with one another regardless of doctrinal truth or
error is more to be deplored. That is a note of our
common contempt for doctrinal truth and our willingness
to compromise everything.

But further, teaching must compel a right attitude
toward God ; and no attitude is right until it produces
worship as its inevitable expression. The preacher
cannot be content till he has this note to authenticate
his ministry, the people in devout worship. Our
Master Himself spoke of His Mission in these terms :
He came to seek and to save the lost, and to seek these
that they might worship in spirit and in truth. It
is by worship that the Body of Christ is unified, and
brought into its true harmonies of fellowship. Worship
is the full response of man to God's Self-disclosure ;
the Creeds themselves are acts of praise because they

acknowledge confidently the truth of revelation. We have not to exhort our people to church attendance; we have rather to teach them the Christian faith and lay upon them the obligation of worship. And worship is not a private transaction; it is the corporate action, the movement and utterance of the great congregation. If our people were accustomed to worship together they would soon learn to work together for the common good; no one can estimate what loss of spiritual power and social health has been caused by our unhappy divisions in religious matters. And the neglect of public worship inflicts upon personal spiritual life an irreparable loss; no man can reckon himself truly in grace whilst he withholds himself from the congregation of Christ's Church in its necessary tribute of worship. "To be cut off from the congregation" was the severest penalty known in the Covenant of works: and this was written for our learning in the Covenant of grace. To be self-excluded from the highest vocation of man upon earth, the worship of God, is to condemn oneself gratuitously to spiritual palsy.

Worship is the right disposition of the person towards God in the concurrence of the fellowship; and it ought to inspire all the social relations. But in these days there is a singularly widespread lack of moral courage amongst Christian people, and men are less ashamed of their sins than of their religion. This is especially true in commercial populations, where much of one's welfare depends upon the goodwill of others. Then a man cannot afford to be singular, or to take a separate course for himself; and it results that personal religion is hidden, overlaid and smothered. Personal religion needs light and air, and society needs the social witness of Christians for their Lord. The preacher must insist upon this; he must teach the people that every member of the Church has a vocation and ministry. He must help all to know that at any moment the challenge may come, and that none must dare to allow it to pass unheeded. It ought to be impossible in this country for any man to swear in decent society, and go unrebuked. It ought to be impossible in this country for any politician to tell a lie publicly, and go uncorrected. It ought to be impossible for any man to assume that he can safely traduce the Christian religion, or blaspheme with impunity. We have a very wholesome dread of hypocrisy, and we fall into the other vice of hiding our religion as though it were a matter of shame. But no timidity or dread of over-statement can discharge us from the duty of social witness. As the children of Israel took possession of Jericho, ascending up every man straight before him, so must the Christian people claim everything for Christ. Every man straight before him in business, and work, and worldly occupation, and politics, and research, and literature, must advance the claim of God, and extend the kingdom of righteousness. Or we consent to a Christianity which has a name to live and is dead.

The ministry that is committed to us as prophets, preachers, and teachers, is wide and complex. We have to exercise a converting ministry, and to edify the faithful, to offer an adequate pastorate to souls in grace, and to guide and inspire men who are living in the social life, neighbours and relatives to half-heathens. For so great a work the preacher himself must be always in training; for his duty demands special preparation and study. Let us take the measure of our task. Our ministry relates to the whole counsel of God in eternity, for we are ministers of the Word, and in the

beginning was the Word which in the fulness of time
was made Flesh and dwelt among us.

It is claimed for Christianity that it issues from God
and is not a human invention or a developed theosophy.
A writer of the eighteenth century attacked the orthodox
position with a book entitled "Christianity as Old as
Creation"; without becoming heterodox we may accept the suggestion of his title. There is no after-
thought in God and no restatement of Divine truth
to meet an unforeseen necessity. The world is the
school of God, and man is being taught by line upon
line and precept upon precept, here a little and there a
little; and though glosses and interpretations and traditions of the elders gathered thick about the Word,
from time to time every plant which the Heavenly
Father had not planted was rooted up. Christianity
was not given abruptly to a world untaught and un-
prepared; nor are we to think of revelation as beginning with any particular theophany or word of prophecy.
The Holy Scriptures contain a record of Divine revelation which culminates in Christ. God Who in old
time spoke unto the fathers in the Prophets by divers
portions and in divers manners in the end of these
days spoke unto us by His Son; and Christ is the fulfilment of all the words of God that sustained patience
and inspired hope in the heart of fallen man.

But the manifestation of God does not begin after the
Son has entered the world; creation itself is a consistent
utterance of God. Our Lord in His early Ministry
claimed the harmony of His words and works as an
attestation of His Divine Embassy; and we must regard the natural order and the spiritual as alike in
origin and in purpose, as the worlds were made by the
Word of God, and the physical universe so far as matter

can convey spiritual intimation, utters speech and certifies knowledge, consonant with the truth as it is in Jesus. There is sometimes a disposition to set the spiritual in terms of harsh contrast with the natural, and sometimes a readiness to allow that the scientific theorist may do as he will with this present world so long as he allows us to hope for another; but we must abate nothing of the claim of God, Maker of heaven and earth, and of all things visible and invisible. We must believe that He created the worlds as He looked upon the Crucifixion, and heard the songs of the Redeemed.

And the Word of the Lord by which the worlds were formed is one with the Word by which man is saved. We cannot conceive of a creation left to itself, or of a race forgotten or ignored by the Creator. And some of the Fathers taught that the continuous communication of God with man was invariably and exclusively through the Divine Son, the Word Who should eventually be made Flesh to tabernacle among us. The originating cause of all things, and of man in the number, is the Word of God; all things were made by Him, and without Him was not anything made that was made. And when disobedience broke the harmony of man with God, and disordered that which God had approved as good, recovery was possible only through the Word. Christian discipleship is obedience to the Word of God, and the man redeemed is the new creation in Christ Jesus.

Every theophany in the older dispensation is a syllable of Divine utterance, and all the experiences of the nations that made up the fulness of time before God sent forth His Son into the world, had their due part in pressing the necessity of the Incarnation, and in schooling man to receive the Word. Amongst the Hebrews a great reverence for the Divine Name promoted the use of phrases in place of that Name, of a precautionary or evasive nature, such as, for instance, the Blessed, the Highest, the Holy One. The Rabbis did not allow the Sacred Name to be used in the synagogue readings, and three terms were commonly employed in this circumlocutory manner in the century preceding the Incarnation; these terms were the *Dwelling*, the *Glory*, and the *Word*. These three are brought together, surely not by accident, in the 14th verse of the first chapter of St. John's Gospel—the *Word* was made Flesh, and *Dwelt* among us, and we beheld His *Glory* as of the only Begotten of the Father, full of grace and truth.

The term Word of God has been by some traced to Philo Judæus of Alexandria. He attempted to harmonize Greek philosophy with Hebrew theology, and scarcely saved himself from Pantheism. He gave great prominence in his system to the term Word of God, and used in that connexion such phrases as *First-born*, *Son*, *Image*. But whilst the language of Philo seems to be like that of the New Testament the idea differs totally from the Christian doctrine of the Incarnation. Nor is it to be supposed that St. John was familiar with the writings of Philo, or had any commerce of thought with Alexandria. What then is the sense in which St. John uses this term, *the Word?* We may find the answer to this question by first noting the order of St. John's writings in the New Testament. His first Epistle preceded his Gospel, and is a doctrinal introduction to that later work. The theme of his Epistle is that Life, that Eternal Life which was manifested unto us in Christ. And the purpose of all his writing is that men may believe that Jesus is the Christ the Son of God, and that believing they may have Life through His Name. *Life* is the constantly recurrent word and the underlying note of this prefatory Epistle of St. John; and in the first phrase of this Epistle, Christ is spoken of as the Word of Life. In his book of the Revelation we read of the tree of Life, the crown of Life, the book of Life, the spirit of Life, the water of Life; and doubtless his phrase, *the Word*, is a contraction of the longer title with which he began, that Word of Life which the Apostles touched and handled. St. John is willing to make use of a term which would identify Christ with the Hebrew conception of the Divine Being, but he uses the term in such a way as to fill it with a higher sense than they knew.

St. John's use of this term identifies Jesus Christ with every Word of the Lord: He is indeed Himself every Word that ever came to the Prophets, and the Word by whom all things were created. He is the full Revelation of God, and every moment of His Revelation is in harmony with every other moment. Sin, that is the conflict of human wills with the Divine will, has destroyed the harmony for a while, and so deferred the realization of the Kingdom of God. Evil, death, darkness, are the products of this disharmony in creation, and the ministry of the Word for the conversion of mankind is engaged in the removal of these products by the restoration of man to his true relations with God.

Our Lord came and preached the Gospel of the Kingdom of God. His Words were sacramental instruments whereby He was conveyed to the hearts of His hearers, and they were an effective means for moulding His hearers into His likeness. Jesus Christ not only ministered but lived, and all His actions in a complete

harmony taught more effectively even than His spoken
Word. The narratives presenting the Lord Jesus are
also Words of the Lord Jesus. The Church so used
the Words, and knew that they were not separable; to
divide, or to set part against part is the work of the
devil. So in the meaning of St. John, when "the Word
of the Lord came" to the Prophets that coming was by
inspiration, and partially, and indulgently, as men were
able to bear it; but in the Incarnation the Word came
in the Flesh, and completely.

In St. John's Gospel we see the Word in action,
not only exposing evil but forcing it to destroy itself
by its violence against good. And this is the Gospel
committed to us as the effective instrument of salvation. The Word of Life is the Word by Whom the
worlds were made; life inherent alone in God is com-
municable in Christ. And Christ is formed in the
soul of man by the Word and the Ministry of the Holy
Ghost. The term *Life*, as used by our Lord, means a
possession that one may have, and a status that one may
attain. It is always the Life, or eternal Life, and dis-
tinctively "the Life of the world to come". That phrase
means not simply a future life, but the spiritual Life,
the endless Life of man with God. One who has gained
that possession or reached that status is in the way to
the city which hath eternal foundations. The Christian preacher exercises a ministry in line with the
imperative Word of creation: he is doing the Father's
Will and finishing His Work.

So high a task is laid upon us, and at this time we
have an opportunity almost limitless. The preacher who
would rise to his commission must prepare himself for
this ministry. The preparation of the preacher is larger
in every sense than the preparation of his sermons;

it must underlie his public addresses and it must be continuous and inclusive. The preacher should aim at becoming an adept teacher, in possession of all the persuasive and impressive methods of the schools. If his lot is cast in a place in which the day schools are closed to him he should seek the opportunity of teaching regularly in some other schools within his district. There can be no sufficient reason for limiting instruction in our day schools to the clergy of those churches to which the schools are attached. It is true that in many cases the teaching of the newly ordained clergy is not of much value to the children, but the result of that ministry upon the clergy themselves is priceless and life-long. The necessity of keeping the attention of sixty or seventy children whilst one is teaching a definite subject from the syllabus for forty-five minutes, is the most direct way of learning to give coherent instruction. Many of our bishops have wisely undertaken the oversight of the sermon preparation of deacons in their dioceses : it is important to limit their preaching, but it is more important to insist upon their systematic teaching in the day schools.

And to school practice it is well to add the frequent making of analyses and the studying of form in the sermons of great preachers and great orators. There are many books which offer briefs or short schemes of sermons and addresses. These may be of some service to the practised speaker, but for the student it is better to accustom oneself to make analyses of sermons and addresses for oneself. Many of the old preachers, like Pepin and Raulin and Tauler and Harpius,[1] have left immense stores of sermons which will afford good subject-matter for analytical study. The student familiar

[1] See Appendix B, p. 205.

with their methods, and conversant with their theology, is already well equipped.   It is not too much to ask of the Christian preacher that he will prepare himself for his work as diligently as the journalist or secretary studies to perfect himself in his business.

To day school instruction and the making of analyses the preacher should add the habit of meditation.   There is nothing else that helps the preacher so much as meditation; by meditation he lays hold upon strength. The Books of the Gospel ought to be worked through systematically in this way, and continually worked through time after time ; a complete course of the four Books should occupy about three years.   The Book chosen for study and meditation should be read first as a whole, and with a critical commentary.   When its characteristics and peculiarities have been learned the Book should then be marked off into short paragraphs. Every paragraph should be a self-contained section, the shortest whole divisions of the Book.   Within the paragraph the verses relate to one another, and have their immediate context in the contents of the paragraph.

In meditation one verse or part of a verse is taken, and this is considered first in reference to the passage in which it stands.   This consideration gives the text its true setting, and pictures the scene or the incident of which it tells.   That is almost wholly a mental process, and requires for its exercise such knowledge as one may derive from Oriental history and archæology and artistic representation.   The student should avail himself of every opportunity and means to focus and visualize the common life of Palestine in the days of our Lord upon earth.

The second part of a meditation is the affectional; it is of the heart rather than of the head.   One cannot rehearse to oneself the least incident in the Gospel story without some responsive movement of affection, as of admiration, of gratitude, of indignation, or wonder. The meditation becomes deeper and more real as it takes up the soul, and one gives oneself wholly to it. And then judgment proceeds upon the informed mind and the kindled affection ; and a definite resolution is made which relates the text to practical life and applies the doctrine to the disciple.

In this complete process head, heart and hand have their several parts in picture, affection, and action. And the daily use of meditation forms a mind and temper of enormous value to the preacher; he builds up his own spiritual life and at the same time discovers the intimate way to the hearts of the faithful in Christ. The devotional study of other parts of Holy Scripture should be made at other times, not intermitting the daily meditations here suggested. It is in the Gospels that one finds the clue to the right understanding of other Scriptures.

Knowledge of the text and of method must be supplemented by knowledge of the people to whom instruction is to be given. The preacher who is not also a pastor suffers a great disadvantage ; for there is no experience that helps in the preparation of sermons so much as ordinary parochial intercourse. In the parish one may see the working out of theories and alternatives that seem to challenge the truth or authority of Christianity ; and one may find in the parish the confirmation of the Gospel. From the people one learns not only how they talk, but, what is more important, how they think. Instruction from the pulpit may be misdirected and consequently ill-received unless the preacher gets his range and elevation from a personal knowledge of the people whom he addresses. The pastor ought to know better than any of the people themselves what course one or another would probably take under conditions of excitement or depression or particular change of circumstances; and from such knowledge he should be able to fortify them beforehand against doubt or dissent or moral disaster.   It is through parochial work that the Divine sympathy for the people is most definitely expressed.   This pastoral ministry of ours is of supreme value to the people, to the Church, and to the pastor. It must be related to the ministry of preaching in action and reaction.   Intimacy with the conditions of life amongst the people gives a quality of human sympathy to instruction and exhortation, and prevents this from being affected and unreal.   And as the marks of the Good Shepherd are two, that He knows His sheep, and is known of them, so the ministry of the preacher will gain as his words are supported and indorsed by personal intercourse with the faithful.

It is undeniable that the charge committed to us as witnesses for Christ and prophets of this day is of immense magnitude.   But with all the shifting circumstances that seem to challenge the truth of revealed religion there is no ground for dismay or despair.   The Christian belief is a new beginning in every generation, and the Christian life a new verification of that belief in every disciple.   And yet, unbroken by successive generations, the Christian tradition runs on, and we are the depositories of that tradition, as well as the voices of that belief.   We must give ourselves to our work with confidence in the Word and the Holy Ghost.   God is not bound by precedents or circumstances, and future ages may see greater achievements in grace than ever the past has known.   No change of social or political conditions can make the ministry of Christian prophecy unnecessary, and every change will give it new opportunity. The Gospel is for the correction and amendment of human life; and those to whom it is committed must be alert and persistent, equipped with Divine learning and resolute to apply it sympathetically through all the provinces of human life. The servant in the Gospel who hid his talent in the ground made his excuse in the character of his master. If we do not misknow ours or mistrust Him we shall use our talents with confidence, and commit the results to Him Who alone can give the increase.

APPENDIX A.

THE following three questions have been addressed to a number of men engaged in active parish work in various parts of England and Wales. Of the answers received the most suggestive are printed in this Appendix.

1. What do you think the strongest ordinary motive amongst your people disposing them to religious denomination, political party, social friendship, etc.: e.g. self-interest, sociability, patriotism, admiration of virtue?

2. What in your judgment most hinders the reception of spiritual truth, e.g. worldly temper, illicit occupations, trade dishonesty, social cowardice?

3. In any case of conversion that has come to your notice what has been the cause or apparent occasion?

J. W.

1. What do you think the strongest ordinary motive amongst your people disposing them to religious denomination, political party, social friendship, etc.: e.g. self-interest, sociability, patriotism, admiration of virtue?

(i) I think the upper and upper-middle classes of England are moved chiefly by idealism to political opinion, or to the particular religious denomination to which they belong; whereas the lower and lower-middle classes are moved more by sociability. Self-interest enters largely into the movements of all those who are closely connected with commerce or trade, less so with the industrial and artisan classes.

(ii) I think a man is *born* a Conservative or Radical; a sacramentalist or non-sacramentalist; an intellectualist or empiricist. Some men of course are not very strongly coloured or flavoured, and so circumstances, home training, etc., may obscure their natural colour. Some are so highly coloured that they would become Quakers in the Vatican or Ritualists in a Scotch manse. Again there are men in whom several strains meet and it is a struggle which predominates. Sometimes to the end of a man's life there is no final solution ; the will is too weak or the nature too rich and complex for any final unification. But "we are as God made us" and the attempt to make a sacramentalist of a Puritan or *vice versa* must fail : or equally to make a Conservative of a Radical.

(iii) Very largely heredity. It is extraordinarily difficult to get them to accept any new point of view.

(iv) I should not say that self-interest is a considerable feature either in the political or religious attachments of my people. Indeed self-interest often lies in other directions. The main factors are, religiously, conviction, early training and sociability ; and politically, idealism and early training.

(v) If by religious denomination is meant this or that sect I have found the dominating influence to be self-pleasing, "I go where I can get what I like ".

(vi) I am desirous of expressing my opinion, to begin with, that the attachment to "party" in religion is not brought about, ordinarily, by the same pressure of motive as that which is at work in politics (and I do not mean of course politics in the Aristotelian sense !).

    (*a*) Let me get politics out of the way by saying that I believe *self-interest* to be in the large majority of cases the prevailing motive at work. We have in the country the continual phenomenon of a man transferring his allegiance from one party to another, because his enemy, supposed or otherwise, is attached to the party in which he himself has hitherto trusted to serve his material interest.

(b) *Religion.*—I deal with this, under this head, absolutely apart from the question of conviction or intellectual assent, and I give as the tip-top motive, in my opinion, obedience to *personal* influence wielded by another.   In the case of the young this is all-but universal.

(vii) Speaking not of village people but of social equals and friends one meets, or I meet—I should say *men* as opposed to the women kind, have been largely alienated from the Church and a more religious life by the dull narrow type of parson that we seem getting everywhere in our country places; they prose somewhat long sermons at their people and from not going to Church (as it comes to) the country gentleman thinks less and less of spiritual things, at any rate in his younger and more active years ; as he becomes an old man I think much of early training exercises a spell over him again, and he is distinctly inclined to religion more, if not (as, alas ! seems so frequent) choked off again by a stupid parson.   I think a large number still go to Church and show an interest in things religious from a good sense of duty.

(a) *Religious Denomination.*—The majority of "religious" people are "what the parents were before them" !   As children they are sent to Sunday schools and places of worship and become associated with that particular form of worship without ever giving the matter any serious thought at all.

(b) *Political Party.*—Mainly self-interest.   "What direct personal benefits shall *I* receive ? "

(viii) This town is in this respect *sui generis*.   It is a town of one industry, and its politics, social ideals and even to some recognized extent its religious denominational adherence are all regulated by the interests of "the Trade". This is a statement of fact that would not, I believe, be questioned by anyone who knows the place well. I think that this is inevitable, as things are. I do not consider that the people are to blame.

(ix) The stream flows strongly towards the Church, as the people learn the truth. Those who remain outside are :—

    (a) Those who have a long and strong family tradition.

    (b) Those who find their gifts or importance not fully recognized or given full play outside the Nonconformist bodies.

Politics have nothing to do with Church and Chapel here, or very little, I am glad to say.

In one part of the parish all the farmers except two are Nonconformists. Some of these use strong measures to secure only chapel-goers as workmen.

(x) It is not possible to give a general answer—for if you take a dozen people who have come over from Dissent to Church you will find no two people with a common experience.

As far as it is possible to speak generally I would say, that as far as Church and Dissent are concerned, the predominant factor in the conversion of a Dissenter to the Church is that of utter weariness and disgust with the incessant dragging in of politics into Dissenting pulpits. When a Dissenter leaves his Chapel for Church, the worship of the latter comes to him as one of the greatest surprises of his life. The reverence, orderliness and beauty of the services strike him as beyond anything he had ever heard or dreamt of.

The difference in doctrine when being prepared for Confirmation also appeals to him—and he finds himself transferred from a system of negations to the joy and freedom of positive truth, as well as from an atmosphere of bickerings to one of peace.

On the other hand, I have known a man—almost an isolated case—to leave the Church and join the Wesleyan body. I found from him that the freer worship and less formal type of service appealed to his particular temperament. He was an ill-instructed Churchman—needless to say.

I am bound to state my own conviction after many years' intimate knowledge of Dissent—that what appeals to many Dissenting minds—particularly the Welsh mind—is the opportunity of taking individual part in the services, i.e. of being asked to pray extempore, and to relate spiritual experiences. As one person told me : " I am somebody in the Chapel, I should be nobody in Church ". The prayer meeting looms large in the system of Dissent.

The question of social friendships as a factor in disposing people to denominations is, of course, a very real one. But as a rule one does not find that it lasts. A young fellow becomes attached to a girl, the man a Churchman, the girl a Baptist. He goes off to the Baptist Chapel with her, and apparently he is lost to the Church. They marry and the children are brought to the Church for baptism. Invariably they are all won back to the Church.

(xi) Custom or tradition.

(xii) Of course the factor which most frequently determines a person's denomination is the early upbringing.

In cases where a person deserts the denomination of his parents the following reasons may be given. Of course I speak chiefly of cases where people have joined the Church of England.

    (a) Sometimes it is a real preference for another denomination, e.g. I have known of people who have come to the sincere conviction that the Church of England is a true branch of the Church, and that the denomination which they are leaving is not. Such cases are, unhappily, not common. More often the preference is due to something which is not so essential; e.g. there is a desire for liturgical worship, or (*per contra*) for extempore prayer.

(*b*) Sometimes a superficial cause is to be traced : e.g. a child is sent to the nearest Sunday school, and sticks to the denomination to which it happens to belong. Or he goes with some friend to some Church or Chapel. Or a young man goes with his sweetheart to her place of worship, or *vice versa*.

(*c*) I have known of cases where people have been repelled by a religion of hate, e.g. one of my best Sunday school teachers had originally been a Congregationalist. She heard the Church so frequently abused that curiosity led her to try the Church. Having tried it she stayed.

(xiii) The line of least resistance explains the denomination of "the many". Anything worthy of the name of conversion, or spiritual crisis, is the experience of the few. I should say advisedly that the average life of to-day goes from the cradle to the grave without anything approaching a serious spiritual struggle. There is very little power of initiative in religion amongst our people. The effort to think out, or make up one's mind, or take independent action is too great for "the majority". In one word the "strongest ordinary motive in disposing persons to religious denomination" (which is what you ask for) is the saving of themselves trouble. And proof positive of this is that the bulk of the people end up by going nowhere to worship, and attaching themselves to no denomination, which is after all the easiest thing to do.

(xiv) Personality of parish priest in religion.

Self-interest in politics.

Tradition, early training counts for much.

I believe people are most often affected by association with others, neighbours, fellow-workers, or relations, A man or woman that has really been reached and rescued will tell others and so it rolls on and gathers volume.

(xv) I think religious denomination is largely determined by the environment of youth.   Most people are what their fathers were, or perhaps rather what their mothers were. But it seems to me that between sixteen and twenty-one there comes to most youths a time of unsettlement, and at the close of this period, according to temperament, they either return to the hereditary denomination *or* take a diametrically opposed position *or* lapse into irreligion.

Political party is less a matter of environment than it used to be.   It is becoming increasingly opportunist and dictated by self-interest and less a matter of principle.

Social friendships are largely governed by community of interests and tastes.   They are also frequently the result of " belonging to the same Church ".

I have meetings with all Dissenting Sunday school teachers and the Church teachers.   Many scholars leave us or them because something irritates them at the moment. E.g., I have just discovered a young man whom I prepared for Confirmation and who says he went away because the teacher nagged at him.   He is attending a Baptist Chapel. Nearly all my adult Dissenting candidates for Confirmation have come to me because there is not enough to satisfy them in their religion, or because prejudices *re* our absence of spirituality have been removed.

Husbands influence wives, and wives husbands.

There is not enough definite teaching either in the Church or in Dissent.

Political party is a fairly strong factor, now getting weaker as Liberals discover that they can be tolerated in the Church.

Self-interest occasionally.

Idealism strong in some cases.

I have always had at least one batch a year of adult candidates for Confirmation and always some of them Dissenters or former Church people attending chapel for a time.

(xvi) My reflections are largely based on nearly eight years in East London (over the border).

Religious Denomination.—There are, no doubt, many loose hangers-on in most congregations. Those who are really "attached" would seem to have been awakened to the meaning of Christian Revelation for themselves, and found a "spiritual home" in the Church. Very often the Christian faith is found to be the satisfaction of the life that is hunting about for something permanent and living. As "desire fails" and interests change, Christ Living and Permanent is realized as the only "secure possession" amid the shifting scenes and changing interests of life. Probably there is less religion of a general sort, because there is less "sentiment," and religion is the result of real inquiry, and has been found by experience to be the "thing that works".

Political Party.—Mainly determined by heredity, business interests or influence at work or at clubs. The ordinary Radical thinks it pays best. The prosperous tradesman and business man is a Radical because he can "shine" among Radicals, whereas he would be a nobody among the Tories.

Social Friendship.—Various causes—some attracted by temperament—some by social position—many find their closest friends (and retain them) at their work and business. There is the strong desire for a confidential friend, which will provide an outlet for expressing their deepest feelings and perplexities and offer an opportunity for the free interchange of ideas.

(xvii) *Strongest motive* disposing to religious denomination lies here, I think, in the fact that their people have been Church people; and if drawn out of their state of absolute indifference, it is the Church that they look to. Our difficulty here does not arise from other denominations, who are doing little, but it is indifference as to everything.

(xviii) The strongest ordinary motive disposing my people to religious denomination, political party, social friendship is undoubtedly the passion for acquiring—the horror of giving. They have no idea of giving, because their whole life is absorbed by a narrow commercialism.

Social friendship they seek which gives most pleasure and is not likely to diminish from the importance in which they are held by the neighbours—there is but little idea of seeking friendship that is likely to make a demand for self-sacrifice.

The political party is supported from which most class-benefit is likely to be derived : or that which is likely to bring most scope for the development of the particular trade or business.

(xix) Replying to the first question I should say :—

    (*a*) The most general motive would be education or environment, by which I mean that men brought up as Church people or Conservatives are likely, when they come to manhood, to continue to belong to the Church or to the Conservative party in the State.

    (*b*) The next motive would probably be the associations of that education or environment, whether pleasant or the reverse ; e.g. if their religious life is associated with happiness it would be continued ; if with restraint and perhaps something of hypocrisy, it would have the effect of making them go into the opposite extreme ; that is, a sectarian would then become a Churchman hating sectarianism ; an English Churchman would become a Romanist.

    (*c*) A motive in many cases would be friendship, the influence of a strong personality at a time when character and opinion were somewhat unformed.

(xx) It is the rarest thing in the world to discover any *conviction* as the determining factor in denomination ; except in the case of Roman Catholics and some instructed

Churchmen.   Accident of birth (especially with Presbyterians), friendships, and the merest chance in the first instance seem to lead to drifting into, rather than choosing, a denomination.

Then they stick to it because changing demands some sort of motive.   This indifference to principles is *proved* by the utter disregard of denomination in the schools, Sunday and day, to which they let their children go.

There are many people who are interdenominational, and the advent of a sensational preacher, or a sufficiently advertised brotherhood or fellowship gathers them to the centre of interest for the time.

(xxi) I fancy the strongest motive which attaches people here to anything is sociability.

(xxii) Does the question centre round the word "disposing"?   Do you mean the new attachment of a man, say in middle life, to a religious denomination, etc.?   If so I answer "pique".   Pique is a form of self-importance if not of self-interest: and the strongest ordinary motives for changing one's opinions are not, as a rule, motives that a man can be proud of.

(xxiii) The strongest ordinary motive disposing to religious denomination is, I think, people's "upbringing" or home training, though this latter seems too strong a word, as too often there is no real training in the home.

To political party again "upbringing".   I know many who belong to some political party simply because Father did.   Self-interest too often has weight, and too seldom national interest.

Social friendship is, I think, greatly determined by similarity of interest.

   2. What in your judgment most hinders the reception of spiritual truth, e.g. worldly temper, illicit occupations, trade dishonesty, social cowardice?

(i) Not so much open hostility as spiritual stagnation, stolid indifference, self-complacent apathy, an utter absence of desire for anything but to be left alone: due perhaps to the deadening force which there is about familiarity, which gradually robs a man of the power to realize: the tendency of the human mind to lose its hold upon the real character of things to which it becomes accustomed.

There is too in many cases a *moral* reason: and the worldly spirit and excessive love of pleasure and excitement is a great hindrance.

(ii) A great number are from lack of training unable to think things out for themselves. I think the rush and hurry to enjoy life and to get all they can out of it selfishly, prevent society people from accepting spiritual truth—people cannot find time to sit down and think of better things, and a great many who really are good at heart and would like to live more religious lives are ashamed to own it.

N.B.—At a big house party nine men one Sunday morning, not long ago, at a house where I stay, at breakfast said they were going to do this and going to do that: the tenth guest, a well-known sporting man, came down late. He was asked what he was going to do and he said, " Oh, I am going to Church, of course ": he did and all the nine went too without saying another word.

(iii) Presuming that the question presupposes the *attractive* presentment of truth, I should unhesitatingly reply that the hindrance to its entrance is self-love in the large majority of cases; the difficulty of applying to the life the great principles involved by the full acceptance of those tremendous facts, which are held to be incontrovertible and therefore to demand intellectual assent. Perhaps I have here misinterpreted the word " reception " in the question.

(iv) First in the list of hindrances to reception of spiritual truth I should place lack of all interest in things spiritual,—

non-belief. Spiritual things do not seem to be the things that matter.

I should think that non-belief in a future life is very widespread.

(v) The chief hindrances to conversion are prosperity and an indifference which fails to distinguish between moral and spiritual standards. The chief hindrance to growth in the spiritual life is the callousness begotten of familiarity with the truth. I do not think that trade dishonesty or social cowardice are factors. Doubtless the social conscience of many needs education, but they are consistent *up to their lights*.

(vi) Here the pressure of economic conditions is a conspicuous difficulty. Alterations of overtime and slackness of work are very demoralizing. And I am struck with the almost entire absence of any effective belief in any future life.

(vii) Noise. There are many coming and going and there is no time so much as to eat bread. Most people have no *time* to hear the message. It always seems to me that the chief cause why people do not accept the Gospel is that they are stupefied with a mass of details of work or pleasure.

(viii) A leading article in the "Times" (of 12 Oct., 1911) maintains that the present generation has been brought up upon the Puritan idea of virtue, and has not inherited any great tradition of austere virtue which is either beautiful or romantic—"Virtue has been made ugly," so says the writer, "not only to the vicious, but to the great mass of ordinary men".

The element of truth in this may account for the wave of materialism through which we have been passing, and to the deplorable fact that a very disproportionate importance is accorded to the opinion of other people as contrasted with what pleases God. The consequence is that both a worldly temper and social cowardice are hindering the reception of spiritual truth.

(ix) 1. Sexual impurity.

2. Indifference.

3. Amongst the rich the chase of exciting pleasures.

(x) I believe that the Established position of the Church is the greatest hindrance to the reception of spiritual truth. Of course "worldly temper, social cowardice, trade dishonesty" are everywhere factors hindering such reception, but I come, reluctantly, to the conclusion that the Church herself, in political and social bondage, with no tests and therefore no sense of membership : treating devout Communicants and the indifferent and notorious sinners all alike : with traditions of worldliness which seem really ineradicable as long as the Establishment lasts,—that the Church herself, acquiescing in and defending a state of affairs which means the practical negation of spiritual religion, is *the* hindrance to the reception of spiritual truth.

Of course a *nucleus* of earnest persons have come out into Catholic freedom.   But the vast majority of my congregation —and of nearly every congregation—is held by the tradition of the Elizabethan "settlement" in Church and State. Their Churchmanship has hardly any connexion with the Christian religion or indeed with any religion.   They equally dislike the Catholic doctrine of grace and the Sacraments, and the Evangelical doctrine of conversion.

(xi) I should put in the first place—indifference.   It is, I find, ever so much easier to attack an open and notorious evil life—a drunkard's, for instance—and hope for some splendid result, than the constant preaching to a congregation many of whom have become Gospel-hardened.   The term Gospel-hardened is no mere figure of speech.   The spirit of receptivity is gone, and it appears that only a miracle of Grace can break up the stony minds and souls.

Then the spirit of worldliness—the caring more for the things of the body than the soul is a terrible hindrance. Religion to these people is confined to the four walls of the Church—and limited strictly to Sunday morning attendance at Church. There they leave it, with their Hymn-book and Prayer Book,—ready to be used on the following Sunday.

To a far larger number, especially among the young, the curse of betting and gambling eats out anything like a desire for spiritual truth—while other sins, freely spoken of and considered as quite common and even necessary, prove a fatal stumbling-block to spiritual receptivity.

In this parish we have not a single publican who attends Church—while many have been buried quite twenty years and more before God intended them to die, having drunk themselves to death. I consider their non-attendance at Church due to the unscrupulous way in which almost without exception their houses are conducted. Any and every trick is resorted to in order to sell their goods and take money.

It is but rarely that we find a man who is a Communicant engaged in a business likely to produce evil or sorrow into other lives. If he does become entangled, he drops his Communions and in this gives up his Church.

(xii) Mainly worldliness or pre-occupation in one pursuit or another, but sometimes honest agnosticism.

(xiii) I should say the worldly temper is the most serious and fatal obstacle to the reception of spiritual truth, even more so than illicit occupation or secret sin. The worldly person seems often to be almost dead in conscience. The sinner's conscience may be awakened but the worldling's is clad in armour of proof. Respectability is the absolute criterion of goodness and if it is coupled with a quasi-philanthropy it is held to include the whole duty of man.

(xiv) I put first of all hindrances pleasure loving and pleasure seeking.

Then some strong passion of sin takes possession and the soul is a captive of the devil.

And next I reckon the miserable conditions of life that some have to suffer, unfit dwelling-houses and starvation wages. This embitters a man and makes him hard and resentful, unable to trust God or man.

And I believe the inconsistencies of professed Christians hinder very many. The outsider cannot always distinguish the true from the false among so-called Christians.

(xv) Decidedly, indifference.

(xvi) "As it was in the days of Noe,—eating and drinking and marrying," with the anxieties, pleasures, and pains, attaching to such things is found sufficient to most minds in the ordinary course of life.

Multiplicity of sects, and inevitable competition between them has placed people in the position of patrons, if they choose to take it, of one religious body or another. The step is easy from being patron of a religious body to becoming patron of a creed, and of what lies behind it—even of God Himself. They have a value fatal to humility, the first condition of learning or receptiveness.

(xvii) Certainly worldly temper. If people are not really converted they do not care for God or the things of God ; and it is the spirit of the world which hinders their conversion.

Of course, fear of man has a great deal to do with it.

(xviii) Worldly temper, I think.

(xix) Ignorance, prejudice, "my ideas," and amongst younger men, impurity, and worldliness.

(xx) Worldly temper is the strongest. Men want to be in the Church with a ticket for heaven and yet serve the world. The price of the aforesaid ticket must not be high or men threaten to give up even formal attendance.

Illicit occupations. The publican rarely attends here (he

used to a good deal at ——), because here he is looked upon as inconsistent if he does.

Self-pleasing, satisfaction of lower passions, etc., is of course a great stumbling-block.

(xxi) *What most hinders ?* An unwillingness to commit themselves, due mostly to want of energy arising not so much from worldly temper as from being overdone, and strain of living in London.

(xxii) The reception of spiritual truth is most hindered in this parish by the all-absorbing stress of competition in the business life. It is business all day and every day from 8 A.M. to 7 P.M. and often very much later. The spiritual side of men is completely paralysed ; there is no *feeling of need* for the spiritual life, and cheap, quick means of transit enable the overworked business man to seek the fresh air of the country for the week-end, or if he has not the energy to go away, he stays in the house the whole Sunday.

Further hindrances to the reception of spiritual truth are :—

> (*a*) Our many divisions. Not a few men in this parish assume the rôle of amused onlooker at religious differences and say, " If the trumpet give an uncertain sound who can obey ? " From this it is almost impossible to move them. They answer one's statements about the English Church by opposing arguments from the Roman side.
>
> (*b*) An extraordinary self-opinionatedness. There is no idea that they may possibly be mistaken. They regard their half-truths and misconceptions as being absolutely infallible.

(xxiii) With regard to your second question I should put :—

> (*a*) Worldliness, and especially covetousness, and under this head would probably come trade dishonesty, which, with men, I have found a very great hin-

13 *

drance. "I should wish to be a consistent Christian, but in my business it is impossible to avoid untruthfulness and dishonesty." I have heard this over and over again from men who were most earnest, and who have said to me, "If I don't misrepresent the quality of the goods or the time when they can be delivered, I cannot get orders. Every other firm does." Of course this applies in some businesses far more than in others.

(b) A life of sin, especially sin against conscience, deadening spiritual faculties.

(xxiv) Not definite evil, nor definite worldly temper is the chief hindrance to the reception of spiritual truth, but the absence of that atmosphere of the Spirit in which faith operates. The unspiritual tone of most of our Church congregations (Chapels worse) acts as a positive hindrance to illumination, which can never be primarily intellectual.

The supreme need is more devotion in our good people, more real power in the spiritual region by the devout communicants ; and above all more intensity of concentration in the public service. This would create the atmosphere in which illumination could come. The unillumined would be bathed in the spiritual waves of influence coming from the truly devout.

As it is in most Churches, especially where fashion is conspicuous, other influences radiate in such force from the worshippers that the directly spiritual is overwhelmed.

(xxv) I do not discover much depth of character, and the apparent shallowness causes an indifference to the reception of religious truth, and also much inconsistency. There are of course many exceptions, but there is little stability in the majority of my people,—at least that is my estimate.

(xxvi) A good many men I think will not come to Communion because they fear they will be converted. It would mean a revolution in their own lives. At the same time they have an honest dread of hypocrisy. The great enemy of religion is respectability. The prevalent idea is that one has to live up to a standard that happens to prevail in the neighbourhood where one lives, and in the society in which one moves. The ideal of the Perfect Life shown by Jesus Christ is lost sight of and so there is no room for penitence and grace.

3. In any case of conversion that has come to your notice what has been the cause or apparent occasion ?

(i) This is a difficult question to answer. The Holy Spirit works in so many different ways, and the cause is so often impossible to define : my experience is that the work of conversion is most often a gradual process, and there are so many contributory causes when once the heart responds to the pleading of the Holy Spirit.

(ii) I do not exactly know what is meant by " any case," and therefore shrink from giving some remarkable individual examples. I shall, however, say off-hand, that *suffering* in some one or more of its myriad forms is most often the cause or apparent occasion of conversion.

(iii) Of sensible conversion I have little experience. I have traced changed lives to clearer information as to the claim of Jesus Christ, and the means whereby it may be met.

(iv) I am not sure that I understand the question. So far as my experience goes conversion begins in a sense of sin, or at any rate dissatisfaction with the present mode of life.

(v) I find it very difficult to say. I have come across very few examples of " sudden conversion ". In a good many cases men have come *back* to religion, often rather slowly.

(vi) I could not answer this question. In every case the occasion differs and in no case is there any adequate explanation. It is a single, unique, spontaneous response of the soul to God the Holy Ghost and can neither be explained nor classified. I daresay this is unscientific and William James would deny it. But *I* cannot see any possible system of classification or explanation in the cases I have met with.

(vii) Any sort of conversion which has come to my notice has been the direct answer to intercessory prayer. The means has been, I think, under God some chance word sown in a sermon or an address upon the ground of a heart prepared for it by discipline.

There seem to be three chief grounds of appeal for conversion in the New Testament—(1) Future and present reward and punishment. (2) The love of God. (3) The corporate life, i.e. with St. Paul " Lie not, . . . for ye are members one of another ". Is the third ground pleaded as it might be ? The value of example. The mediatory power of goodness, as in such a passage as " the earnest expectation of creation waiting for the revealing of the sons of God ".

I am sure in a slum parish, there is best hope of winning fathers and mothers through the children.

(viii) Lasting results alone considered, i.e., real conversion.

(1) Confirmation preparation.

(2) Answer to prayer opening eyes to God's love and need of response to it.

(3) Sermons. Not many cases, but enough to tabulate.

(4) The call of sickness, few staunch after full recovery.

(ix) (1) The sense of sin and its intolerable burden.

(2) The desire of protection and guidance in life.

Conversions have usually been the results of special Mission efforts. They have in most cases been lasting in their results.

(x) I have known several striking conversions in this parish, the circumstances of each of which appeared to have nothing or little in common with the others.

(*a*) A man of about 45, the father of a large family,
with a more or less thriftless and intemperate wife,
had been Confirmed in his early days, but had altogether ceased from Church-going and had not
made a Communion for thirty-two years. He
came to Church one Sunday evening, and went
home to pray for the first time in many years.
He came to see me: he is to-day the superintend-
dent of one of our Sunday schools and a most
earnest Church worker. His wife does not appear
to have changed. I cannot say what led this man
to seek a new life, one can only attribute it to the
secret working of God's Spirit.

(*b*) An old man, 70 years of age, who had led a most
dissolute life, and whom I had known for a great
many years, came, quite on his own, and asked to
be prepared for Confirmation. He comes regularly
to confession before each Communion. In this
case I think it was the absolute disappointment in
the bitterness of a life of sin which moved him to
seek his peace with God. He is very poor, and
has much trouble with the old temptations, but is
happy and holds on splendidly.

(*c*) Another man—a terrible drunkard—with the craving
of drink so strong upon him that nothing seemed
possible to save him. Suddenly—quite suddenly
—he seemed to have power given him to master
the temptation. This was *before* he came to
Church: but after he had ceased drinking he asked
to be prepared for Confirmation, and is now a
Communicant. He still has the craving—or rather
a terrible thirst—but he has no desire to quench
it with anything stronger than water.

(*d*) Another case of a terrible drunkard was made known
last week. He had been in jail several times—but
the change came a year ago last Christmas. I

asked him how it came about and he told me the story. One of his sons is a deaf and dumb mute —this boy I succeeded in getting into a school for mutes some ten years ago. On Christmas Day, 1909, the boy was home for his Christmas holidays. The father had been out drinking the whole morning and came home about 3 o'clock more or less drunk. The mother, with her five children and the deaf and dumb boy, was sitting in the kitchen crying. They had had no dinner—and when he came in, the sight drove him nearly mad. His tears were soon mingled with theirs—and he vowed to God that he would never look upon such a sight again. From that day he has never touched a drop of anything intoxicating.

(xi) Speaking of conversion—I have found here that many a man has been entirely changed in his life and ways by his fellow-workman. When you have got one really good Christian working man he will do more than twenty parsons. We have six or eight men here who, humanly speaking, owe entirely to a working man the fact that they are regular Communicants, Sunday school teachers, and the stay of the religion of the place.

Men in society, I mean the country gentlemen rather, are much better than on the surface they seem to be. I think round here, at any rate, the working man has just passed the stage of being sick of political dissent and is moving back a little to the Church.

(xii) Chief cause of conversion : Personal dealing, the response to the personal appeal to yield the will to Christ.

(xiii) I can only attribute conversions I have come across to the secret guiding of the Holy Spirit awakening souls to the reality of the goodness of God, and the saving Power of the Redeemer's love.

(xiv) Though it sounds a dreadful thing to say, one really does not see or expect to see any sudden or marked change in the people with whom I have to deal; it is usually silent and gradual. And I think perhaps preaching has still some power in this direction.

(xv) Conversions coming under my notice are due, I believe, to a grasp of the mystery of the Incarnation as an introduction to the Passion (not *vice versa*). The preaching of the Cross has become a familiar, expected, and unreal thing. Not so, I think, to nearly the same extent the preaching of the Incarnation. Minds which are able to grasp the latter are in the way to realize in themselves the power of the Gospel.

(xvi) The apparent *occasion* of conversion.
I think the time of preparation for Confirmation is often the occasion. It forces young people, at an impressionable age, to think seriously. The grace of Confirmation finishes what is already begun.

A special mission may offer the occasion. It has been a time of real prayer, and people who have been on the brink of making a change in their life are really glad of the opportunity, and come to a point.

Of course, some special event in the house—the sickness of a child, etc., may be the occasion of conversion.

(xvii) Conversion to the Church.
Sincerity in search of truth: and amongst our working people here earnest work and love of souls on part of the Clergy.

(xviii) Personal influence—either of Clergy or workers: these I believe are primary or root impulses which attract different people and make them willing to place themselves in the right environment where they can be taught and have the dormant religious instinct developed,

(xix) In my experience disgust and disappointment of worldly pleasures turns many to God in repentance. Suddenly the eager race after amusements is checked by a feeling of nausea and loathing for the folly and worthlessness of it all, and a true conversion may come then as a reaction.

And I find many persons who have been really converted by being present at the Lord's Supper, without participating. They have been moved by the solemnity of the service, and then they have been broken down by the consciousness that they had no place themselves in the family life of the Christian household. That has brought them up suddenly and overwhelmed them with repentance and a desire to know God.

(xx) In many cases the interior cause has been a real desire to escape from sin (rather than a " fear of the wrath to come ") and from the loss of self-respect entailed thereby. It is difficult, if not impossible, to give any general exterior causes. Personal influence, I should think, is the cause in very many cases. The only really genuine case of conversion of a middle-aged man (45-50) I can recollect was due to personal striving, long-continued, of a priest with the subject.

(xxi) (1) Love of the real truth about the Incarnation. The strongest and most abiding and satisfactory reason.

(2) Result of teaching the whole scheme of the Catholic Church has converted many by its reasonableness and scientific effectiveness. I have a man who plainly told me a while ago that he had been on the verge of going to Rome because no satisfactory scheme seemed to be in our Church. He is a fine working man (a plumber) and he has brought half a dozen other men to church from all sources, some of whom are weekly Communicants now and some are regular at any rate once a day at matins or evensong. He has failed to bring others because they are not keen enough about the truth.

(xxii) The most noticeable conversions that have come to my notice have been those caused by a tremendous reaction from a state of deadly sin indulged in for some length of time. The spiritual eyes have been opened—I should say through the illuminating knowledge of the love of God on Calvary. Gratitude has a large part, I think, in such phenomena.

(xxiii) Paternal love. I had a case of a man of about 40 coming forward for Confirmation with his eldest boy. He felt he must set him the example. This was two years ago, and he has been most regular at his Communion—joined Bible Class, C.E.M.S.—has become a sidesman, and works for the Church. He gives every sign of progress in the life of sanctification.

Another case I know of conversion was brought about by the shame felt at my seeing the man in question drunk. He resolved never to touch drink,—after a year's abstinence signed the pledge,—was Confirmed and became a regular Communicant and is a worker for the Church.

In another case the conversion, humanly speaking, was brought about by intercessory prayer. I told a man I was seeking to get hold of for Confirmation that I felt sure he would come at least to my class, because I had been praying for him. "What, pray for me!" he said, and I never saw any man so touched and astonished. This was at the first class which I had asked him to attend, and at the end, he whispered to me, as he went out, "I have no doubts now".

I have found that to tell lads I pray for them has a wonderful effect.

(xxiv) The cases of conversion that I have observed have been usually somewhat as follows :—

The individual has in the first instance been extraordinarily ignorant of the elements of Christianity : it has been ignorance and misunderstanding or prejudice rather than deliberate wickedness. He has at first very casually and from curiosity drifted into Church for evening services on

Sundays.   His visits to the Church have become more frequent, he is at last interested by what he hears and sees, finally he comes into personal contact with one of the clergy of the Church, who brings him to the point of definite determination, and he is prepared, Baptized, Confirmed and Communicated.   In these circumstances he is invariably ready to make his confession.

(xxv) Conversions here are very, very rare outside such things as missions when this intensity of spiritual atmosphere is really in some measure attained.   This has been my experience here and in New Zealand that it is the discovery of God in the midst that is the chief converting force.

(xxvi) Here they seem to see suddenly the result of a sinful kind of life:—desire to get away from that has, I think, been the cause,—in the few instances I can immediately call to mind.

(xxvii) With regard to the third question it would be impossible to lay down any rules.   "The wind bloweth where it listeth, . . . so is every one that is born of the Spirit."   I have, of course, had the experience of hundreds of cases of real conversion in the forty years of my ministry.   They have come from the most varied causes.   Perhaps the most frequent has been the influence of a strong Christian personality, the influence, for instance, of a priest of magnetic power and great gifts, though I have known the most trivial circumstances to be the apparent beginning of a real conversion.

(xxviii) There are few conversions—but these, I think, are usually due to a gradual perception of Catholic Truth.   Those due to emotionalism do not come under my notice usually.

APPENDIX B.

William Pepin, a French preacher of the fifteenth century : he was Court preacher to Francis I. His sermons had immense circulation, and were printed again and again in Paris and Venice and Lyons. Some of his works were of the character of expositions whilst others were doctrinal and for special occasions. In one book he published fifty-three sermons on one text, Revelation v. 1. He set out his sermons with clear plan and illustrated them very fully from Holy Scripture. He died at Evreux in 1532.

Jean Raulin, a French preacher, born in 1443 ; his ministry was almost entirely in Paris. His Advent and Lent sermons were very famous, and were republished again and again. He used extraordinary minuteness of division and subdivision. His knowledge of Scripture lights up all his sermons, and, whilst his style is too elaborate to be copied, much may be learned from his application of Scripture to Scripture, and elucidation of mystical meaning.

John Tauler, a German of the Dominican Order, born in 1290 : he was a prolific writer and his works have passed through many editions. There is little plan in his sermons and their note is one of subjective piety. But much may be learned from the leading ideas of his preaching, the intimacy of the soul with God, and the love between Christ and the soul. His sermons are not to be taken by us as models for the preacher, but they should be studied for what they suggest of spiritual instruction.

Henry Harpius, a Flemish preacher, born in 1478 : he was a mystic with a right deference for scholastic theology, quoting St. Thomas Aquinas and Peter Lombard frequently. He wrote his sermons with definite structure, an introduction well worked out, and the sermon itself with marked divisions. His precise and deliberate method makes his work peculiarly useful for the modern preacher.

INDEX.

Increase of emotionalism, 12.
Individual instruction, 111.
Inducements to attend services, 83.
Industry and commerce, 90.
Infection of grace, 99.
Influence of environment, 58.
Informal talks on religion, 118.
Inspiration not imitation, 131.
Institutional Church, 6.
Intercourse with the Holy Ghost, 138.
Interpretation of Scripture, 76.

JAPANESE artist, 21.
John Wesley on preaching, 73.

KINGSHIP accidental and subordinate, 35.

LACK of moral courage, 168.
Lack of Scriptural knowledge, 136.
Law before Gospel, 45.
Learning from scholars, 112.
Learning to learn, 149.
Legitimate succession in family religion, 62.
Lent and Advent courses, 152.
Liddon in St. Paul's, 14.
Life eternal and heavenly, 174.
Life not literature, 134.
Local climate in religion, 96.
Local Dissent, 7.
Loss of arts and crafts, 8.
Loss of domestic tradition, 144.
Loss of home life, 12.
Loss of spiritual sense, 48.

MAKING of analyses, 175.
Man natural and man spiritual, 22.
Manner of the preacher, 63.
Mediation of Christ, 34.
Mental fertility, 107.
Mental knowledge of Scripture, 108.
Mind of the Church, 75.
Mind of the crowd, 55.
Ministry from without, 44.
Ministry of exhortation, 85.
Ministry of restraint, 40.
Ministry of St. John Baptist, 23.
Miracle at Cana, 26.
Mission instruction, 157.
Mission methods, 156.
Mission of the Church, 37.
Missions or revivals, 115.

Misuse of word Church, 127.
Modern journalism, 95.
Monothelite heresy, 26.
Moral disorder in England, 101.
Moral indisposition, 97.
Moral notes of sex, 124.
Moral predisposition, 71.
Moral results of public disasters, 12.
Mystical Body of Christ, 127.
Mystical understanding, 142.

NATHANAEL claimed by Christ, 31.
Natural predispositions for the spiritual, 30.
Necessary affinity, 69.
Necessary consciousness of sin, 117.
Need of detachment, 29, 42.
Need of personal decision, 27.
Need of spiritual instruction, 165.
Need of true standards, 45.
Nicodemus a disciple, 20.
Normal human life, 125.
No succession of separate Apostles, 38.
Note of the preacher, 57.

OBLIGATION of fellowship, 129.
Obligations of Baptism, 163.
Opportunities of modern life, 14.
Other-worldliness, 78.

PARABLE of the Sower, 1.
Parent and child, 99.
Parish Conventions, 153.
Parochial godparents, 146.
Parochial intercourse, 177.
Parochial prayers, 150.
Pastoral not social, 113.
Pastoral sympathy, 178.
Pastoral visitation, 113.
Perception and reflection, 57.
Perils of the letter, 133.
Period of adolescence, 109.
Personal assent, 76.
Personal bias, 98.
Personal character, 94.
Personal character made by volitions, 2.
Personal confidence in God, 22.
Personal conviction, 27, 32.
Personal crisis, 123.
Personal gambit, 106.
Personal influences, 70.
Personal responsibility for belief, 61.

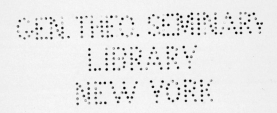

ABERDEEN : THE UNIVERSITY PRESS.